LOCOMOTION PAPERS

The
Wye Valley
Railway
and the
Coleford Branch

by

B.M. Handley & R. Dingwall

THE OAKWOOD PRESS

First published 1982
Reprinted 1983
Reprinted 1988
Second Edition 1998
Revised Second Edition 2000
Third Edition 2007

British Library Cataloguing in Publication Data
A Record for this book is available from the British Library
ISBN 978 0 85361 665 8

Typeset by Oakwood Graphics.
Repro by PKmediaworks, Cranborne, Dorset.
Printed by Cambrian Printers Ltd, Aberystwyth, Ceredigeon.

A view of Tintern station looking towards Monmouth. This photograph dates from the mid-1960s, the track and sleepers are in the process of being removed. Tintern station now has a teashop in the old waiting room, with exhibitions housed in the old signal box, the 10 acre site is now a picnic and conservation area. You can relive a journey along the Wye Valley line through a DVD presentation housed in one of the static carriages which also contains a small historical display of the railway. *Pat Kedward Collection*

Title Page: Wye Valley Railway boundary post. *B.M. Handley*

Front cover: An oil painting of Tintern station by Michael J. Tunnicliffe. A GWR diesel railcar waits to depart for Chepstow while a northbound goods train stands alongside.

Published by The Oakwood Press (Usk), P.O. Box 13, Usk, Mon., NP15 1YS.
E-mail: sales@oakwoodpress.co.uk
Website: www.oakwoodpress.co.uk

Contents

Ex-GWR pannier tank No. 6417 enters Redbrook-on-Wye station.   *E. Wilmhurst*

A splendid portrait of fisherman James Edwards near Monmouth *c*. 1910. In the background the railway bridge designed by Joseph Firbank, and constructed in 1860 for the Coleford, Monmouth, Usk & Pontypool Railway can be clearly seen.   *Monmouth Museum*

'You should have seen the one that got away!' Salmon fishing in the swirling waters of the River Wye, with Bigsweir bridge in the background.   *R. Dingwall*

Chapter One

The Source

Plynlimon, at a height of 2,468 ft (752 metres) is not a prominent mountain compared with Snowdon, which stands at 3,560 ft (1,085 metres), indeed, as the names signifies, it has divided its energy to form five separate peaks, none of which is particularly dramatic to distinguish it from its neighbours. More important environmentally is the fact that the Plynlimon range has become a vast catchment area for most of the rain which falls on Wales. The bleak and barren region north of Devil's Bridge seems to live under a permanent black cloud which has turned the grassy ground into a morass which has less consistency than a wet sponge. Praise be that it is here on Plynlimon's eastern flank that two of Britain's famous rivers, the Severn and Wye, find their source within a very short distance of each other. The Rheidol flowing into Aberystwyth is also born on the mountain, together with many un-named streams which babble in different directions to merge further on down the hillside.

Similar to the little rivulets, the Severn and Wye go on their separate courses only to unite after a distance of some 150 miles. The waters of the River Wye, which take a more direct route, finally make an estuary with the broader River Severn at Chepstow. For much of its upper reaches the Wye is essentially a Welsh river, and is known as the Afon Gwy, here the silent, still waters drift lazily along through pleasant pasture land. In this area the Wye plays an important part in the Welsh Marches. Going south, Llangurig, Rhayader and Builth Wells are the major towns the Wye passes through, before the river turns abruptly north-east heading to Hay-on-Wye and so into England. Continuing, the river turns again to visit Hereford, before regaining its southern route, going into Ross-on-Wye and entering the gorges at Symonds Yat.

Around Monmouth the River Wye flows into the Lower Wye Valley, an area of outstanding natural beauty. At this point the river starts to meander between steeply wooded banks to find its way through ancient Siluria, now the border between Monmouthshire and Gloucestershire. By Newland in the Forest of Dean there is an excellent example of a dried up river valley, best seen from the Kymin, where the Wye decided to take a more direct path at some era in time, before continuing to Tintern.

Down stream the remaining short stretch of river runs against limestone cliffs, making several horseshoe bends (these are best seen from Eagle's Nest viewing point at Wyndcliff) before gushing past Chepstow Castle and pouring into the River Severn by the old bridge. For several miles the final section of the River Wye is tidal, and just like the River Severn, a bore can be witnessed at various times. This has occasionally reached over 2 ft in height and can make a tremendous roaring noise as it rushes up the valleys. In season fishermen can often be seen standing in thigh-high waders never knowing if the salmon they are seeking is just lurking between their feet. This is also the home of the elver, the three inch baby eels which migrate from the Sargasso Sea each spring, a traditional journey which takes three years to complete. And so the river goes on forever.

The three Harold Stones at Trellech.   *R. Dingwall*

The Buckstone is to be found at Staunton. In earlier times this huge rock used to wobble back and forth like a see-saw on its narrow base. That was until one day in 1885 when it suddenly rolled down the hill, coming to a halt about 40 ft away. The 45 ton stone was later returned to its original site, this time held much more securely than before.   *R. Dingwall*

Chapter Two

Communication Cords

An examination into the complicated travel arrangements through the ages from Monmouth to Chepstow reveals a varied assortment of transport which was either affected by the natural landscape or the technology of the times. The movement of commodities and people from one place to another were the main considerations which influenced the development of the communication channels.

The earliest tracks connecting Monmouth (King Arthur's Cave area) south towards Chepstow avoided the River Wye and its heavily forested slopes, keeping to the high ground west of the valley. Along the trail, tribes of Silures built several settlements, at Trellech three standing stones can be found in a field. They are called the 'Harold Stones', after King Harold, but obviously date back to much earlier times. The three pillars are formed of conglomerate or pudding stone. They are aligned in a south-west to north-east direction, possibly along a ley line towards the Buckstone and the Longstone at Staunton near Coleford, and on to May Hill and Welshbury, ancient strongholds.

When the Romans came they established forts at Caerleon and Usk, with outposts at Blestium (Monmouth) and Striguil (Chepstow), both of which were vital river crossings (much later, castles were built to protect these towns). It is possible that ores from the area went northwards in galleys to Ariconium (north-east of Ross-on-Wye), where, it is said, the Romans minted coins. Meanwhile legionnaires marched over the ever widening paths between the strategic sites.

In those days the population trekked from village to village with their chattels searching for better land on which to grow food and to hunt. The River Wye provided plenty of fish to catch. Pack horses would have carried the heavy loads until the muddy roads were improved to take carts.

After Roman governance waned, many battles were fought in the locality between those of Celtic tongue and the encroaching Anglo-Saxons, this culminated in the building of Offa's Dyke, which wanders about on the hilltops to the east of the River Wye. This was possibly a demarcation line between the two races rather than a defensive position.

The next invaders to arrive in the region were the Vikings, whose longboats would have easily nudged aside the local fishermen's coracles, to contest the strong currents on the River Wye. These striking craft would have easily reached Monmouth, firstly carrying out raids and later to establish trade.

When the Normans came they left their mark on the Wye Valley in a much more peaceful way. While the bloody battles to subdue the wild Welsh nation were being fought further afield, the foundations of a Cistercian abbey were being laid at Tintern in 1131. The fledgling monastery soon attracted many monks to contemplate God's message of everlasting love and to fulfil their religious vows in the tranquil surroundings. As the abbey expanded numerous high ranking people of state, including King Edward II in 1326, visited the monastic order, others stayed longer and were buried in the grounds.

The Longstone at Staunton. According to folklore, if you prick the rock with a pin at exactly midnight on the summer solstice the stone will bleed.
R. Dingwall

The Devil's Pulpit stands on a hilltop ridge in front of a natural amphitheatre beside the Offa's Dyke path. *R. Dingwall*

Water power was harnessed to turn the wheels of industry along the Wye Valley *R. Dingwall*

The remains of a furnace site in the Angidy Valley at Tintern in 1997. *R. Dingwall*

Tintern became a crossing point on the River Wye, even today, at low tide, stone piers can be traced jutting out from either bank to mark the location. As the Cistercians began to grow and prosper, mainly by their agricultural skills and advanced farming methods, the local townsfolk benefited as well by selling merchandise to the religious community. So it was that the monks became a powerful force within the country, they had a great influence on the affairs of the realm, until, that is, they were disbanded by King Henry VIII when he decreed the Dissolution of the monasteries in 1536.

With the abbey destroyed, life in the district still continued to flourish, especially in the Forest of Dean, by the felling of trees for the King's navy. This enterprise was swiftly followed by the discovery of all the necessary elements, fuel (coal and timber) plus water power, and minerals, to start a smelting industry in the Wye Valley. Noisy, smoky furnaces transformed iron, copper and lead into useful products.

Most of the forges were built along the Angidy Valley. It was on this tributary that a successful wireworks was established, which was to last over 300 years and lead eventually to the building of a tramway and a railway to serve its needs. Osmond Iron was made to produce the finest wire. It is hard to believe today, but brass was first manufactured in Great Britain at Tintern in 1568.

Most of the activities recalled today of the Civil War, as it ebbed and flowed along the Wye Valley, concern Sir John De Wintour. He seemed to have led a charmed life crossing the river many times in the fighting. He finally gave his name to the spectacular 'Wintour's Leap' cliffs near Woodcroft. It is said that he escaped capture from the chasing Parliamentary soldiers by forcing his horse to leap 200 feet over the steep precipices at this part of the river, and plunged into the waters of the Wye below. None would dare follow, and so De Wintour lived to fight another day.

By this time trows were sailing up and down the river, these flat-bottomed boats being ideally suited for navigating shallow water. Shipments of timber, coal and limestone blocks were dispatched to Bristol and Gloucester. Wines and spirits were the cargoes going up stream as return loads. Many trows were built at Brockweir. It is said that Nelson enjoyed sailing trows on the River Wye at Monmouth. William Wordsworth also travelled by trow when he visited the Wye Valley in 1793, and immediately fell in love with the area. He was deeply moved by the romantic and picturesque appeal of the river.

Another contemporary of this period was William Gilpin who wrote his best selling guidebook *Observations on the River Wye* in 1782. The book was probably one of the main reasons that 'tourists' started coming to the area. The numbers of visitors were no doubt swelled due to the war against Napoleon. The offspring of the wealthy could no longer enjoy 'The Grand European Tour' to complete their education, and so instead journeyed to the Wye Valley to seek inspiration. The romantics stayed in the many newly-built inns and hotels which quickly sprang up to cater for their needs.

As the area became even more popular, a turnpike road was finally built in 1826 to cope with all the visitors. This connected Monmouth and Chepstow, following the meanderings of the river, a toll house levied fees at Bigsweir.

Chepstow Castle.   *R. Dingwall*

Monmouth Castle, now home of the Royal Monmouthshire Royal Engineers. It was the birthplace of King Henry V.   *R. Dingwall*

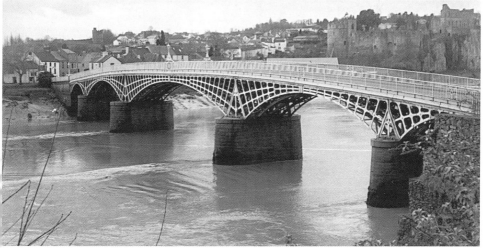

Top: The old bridge over the River Wye at Chepstow.
Chepstow Museum

Above: The new bridge over the River Wye at Chepstow, with the castle in the background.
R. Dingwall

Left: Monnow bridge at Monmouth is the last of four gateways that used to protect the outlying defences.
R. Dingwall Collection

The 31-ton steamboat *La Belle Marie* at Brockweir Quay.   *Monmouth Museum*

Bridge crossing the Wye at Brockweir in May 1978. Brockweir Halt was just to the right-hand side of the bridge.   *B.M. Handley*

The tollhouse at Bigsweir bridge. *R. Dingwall*

An early photograph of Redbrook taken before 1876, possibly viewed from Chapel Lane (*see photograph page 58*). The valley would soon echo to the sound of hissing steam and tooting whistles. *R. Boycott*

With the whole valley opened up to view, stage coaches and charabanc tours were quick to follow the easier route. A climb to the Devil's Pulpit at Tintern enabled legs to be stretched before heading home again.

In 1832 another religious community anxious to save sinners began to take root in the Wye Valley. The Moravian movement first practised in what is now the Czech Republic and gradually through its missionaries, the word of God spread, even to Brockweir. A Moravian church was established to bring the message to those souls in the area, especially those working in the paper mills at Whitebrook or in the wood-turning industry at Llandogo.

At Brockweir shipbuilding was the main source of employment, together with those men in the barge trade. It was by the quay that merchandise would be transferred from seafaring trows onto barges for towing up river by teams of 10 men, often going as far as Hereford. Goods going downstream would be transferred in the same fashion. It was thirsty work, there were 16 pubs to serve the 350 inhabitants and itinerant sailors, but no place of worship until the Moravians built their church on the site of the local cock-fighting pit. The congregation swelled and a school was started in the village.

It was in May 1874 that construction work began on the Wye Valley Railway. The line passed Brockweir on the opposite bank of the river. The rough and tough navvies were ferried across the Wye to attend special gospel services, those present were apparently most orderly and devout at meetings.

The Moravian church at Brockweir. Flora Klickmann, who wrote many wonderful books about life in the Wye Valley (*see page 133*), is buried here. *R. Dingwall*

Chapter Three

Promotion and Construction

There were several sound commercial reasons for promoting a railway between Monmouth and Chepstow, the most obvious was to capitalise on the freight and passenger trade that needed to travel between the two towns. Prior to the opening of the Wye Valley Railway the Victorian traveller or businessman had certainly experienced the great way round. The only link by rail was to travel in a south-westerly direction on the Coleford, Monmouth, Usk and Pontypool Railway (*see Appendix Two*) and then go via Pontypool and Newport to reach Chepstow, making a journey of some 43 miles. The new line proposed a direct route shortening the distance to just 15 miles. By reducing the distance to Chepstow this consequently made access to Bristol all the more easy. The advantage to commerce, industry and the travelling public was obvious. It was also evident that the railway was a popular and welcomed venture with the local communities along the Wye Valley as the following extract from the *Monmouthshire Beacon* on 21st October, 1876 reported:

> Whilst opening up a new district hitherto unapproached by railway traffic, the new line will prove a great convenience not only to the locality through which it runs, but to the travelling public at large and in point of time it will shorten the journey to Bristol by two hours.

The promoters already realised the potential of the Severn Tunnel project and the possibility that the Wye Valley line could play a major role in carrying through traffic from Bristol to the North of England and vice versa. 'The gradients and curves of the line are good, the line having been constructed with the idea of accommodating the through traffic from Bristol to the North of England' reported the *Monmouthshire Beacon*.

'Statement of gross traffic per annum £36,779 does not include any estimate of revenue received by traffic passing over the line on completion of the Severn Tunnel now being constructed' stated S.H. Yockney, FGS, M.Inst.CE, in his report of 24th March, 1874.

The proposed railway would also be a prime factor in the development of Chepstow as a port receiving merchandise direct instead of playing second fiddle to Swansea, Cardiff and Newport. The *Illustrated London News* in October 1876 recorded that 'The port of Chepstow at the southern end of the line may now by means of this new railway become a competing port'.

Another very important but seasonal source of revenue was to be expected from the ever increasing tourist trade encouraged by the beauty of the Wye Valley area. For the Victorian sightseer the new line would provide superb views of the Wye Valley and its surrounding countryside, an exclusive panorama to be observed at will, from the armchair comfort of the railway carriage.

The necessity for a railway had to be proved before public money could be found, or Parliament persuaded to give the necessary authority but with such a

The entrance to Tidenham tunnel from the south.   *The Illustrated London News*

The north end of Tidenham tunnel.   *The Illustrated London News*

wealth of positive research to back the project the promoters confidently presented their plans before Parliament.

Plans were first drawn up for a railway to run between Chepstow and Monmouth in 1865. It was proposed that the line should run along the Welsh west bank of the river; this would have meant that the railway would have passed through Tintern village and not around it, as eventually happened. The Wye Valley Railway Bill was presented before a Select Committee of the House of Lords on 13th July, 1866; the proceedings were chaired by the Earl of Romeny and Mr Mereweather heard the opening case for the promoters. Mr Charles Baker, a Solicitor acting for the Duke of Beaufort, was questioned by Mr Cripps and Mr Grenville Somerset, Queen's Counsellors acting on behalf of the Parliamentary Committee. On cross-examination Mr Baker reported that two-thirds of the land required by the railway belonged to the Duke of Beaufort; this consisted of some eight to ten miles of the total route mileage. It transpired that there was no problem in acquiring this necessary land as the Duke of Beaufort was in complete favour of the railway.* An objection was brought up by the Parliamentary Committee regarding damage to the ancient site of Tintern Abbey. Mr Baker replied that there would be no danger to the abbey or its surrounding boundaries.

The cross-examination then continued with Lieutenant Colonel Willoughby S. Rook of the Scots Fusiliers Guards and Magistrate for Monmouth. Col Rook was also owner of the Bigsweir and Kynaston Estates which were situated part in Gloucestershire and part in Monmouthshire. Along with the Duke of Beaufort's, the Colonel's was all the property that was proposed to be taken by the Wye Valley Railway Company. Col Rook had no objection to the railway. When questioned about his preference of gauge i.e., the Stephenson gauge of 4 ft 8½ in., or the Brunel gauge of 7 ft 0¼ in., he was impartial to whatever gauge was to be used. His non-committal reply was most likely due to the fact that he was unaware of the importance attached to the choice of gauge. Had the 7 ft 0¼ in. broad gauge been used it would have certainly caused problems at Wyesham, situated at the northern end of the line and the Wye Valley Junction at the southern end, as these two places operated on the standard gauge. (This gauge was also referred to rather mockingly by Brunel as the colliers' gauge.)

This break of gauge situation had occurred not far from the Wye Valley at Gloucester in the early 1840s where the Bristol and Gloucester Railway (broad gauge) had met the Birmingham and Gloucester Railway (standard gauge); the annoyance and aggravation caused here brought the whole question of gauge to a head and eventually did much to bring about Parliamentary intervention. A three man committee was formed known as the Gauge Commission, consisting of Lieutenant Colonel Sir Frederick Smith, first Inspector General of Railways of the Board of Trade, George Riddell Airy, Astronomer Royal and Peter Barlow, Professor of Mathematics at the Royal Military Academy, Woolwich. After close scrutiny of the railway gauge situation the Committee decided in favour of Stephenson gauge. This was made official by the Gauges Act of 1846 which forbade the construction of non-standard gauge railways, but

* In 1872 the route was altered to run east of the river by-passing Tintern. The Duke was so annoyed that he insisted upon a goods branch crossing the river (*see page 141*).

made an exception for extensions to existing broad gauge railways situated mainly in the West Country.

The Act was really the final blow to Brunel's much loved broad gauge. The second broad gauge to standard gauge conversion took place near Monmouth on a 22½ mile stretch of line between Grange Court and Hereford on the Hereford, Ross and Gloucester Railway in August 1869. (The first conversion was the Aylesbury branch in October 1868.)

There had been some opposition to the Wye Valley Railway Bill on its initial reading because of the proposed broad gauge construction, but the opposition was dropped when it was confirmed that standard gauge track was to be used. When the question of land and gauge had been successfully debated the Committee then moved to the next stage, that of engineering and estimated cost of construction. Mr William Henry Lefevre (Civil Engineer) was working on the project in conjunction with S.H. Yockney & Son of Westminster, who were the official Engineers, and had carried out the initial survey. Mr Lefevre reported that the estimated cost had been set at £222,298 for 14½ miles of line from the GWR junction known as the Wye Valley Junction to Monmouth, and that the steepest gradient would be 1 in 71 for six furlongs. Two tunnels were to be built, one estimated to be 249 yards long and the other an estimated length of 715 yards.

The Wye Valley Railway Bill managed to get a successful reading and Parliament sanctioned the line on 10th August, 1866. It was incorporated under the Wye Valley Railway Act (29 & 30 Vict. cap. CCCLVIII) and (34 & 35 Vict. cap. XLLX) with a share capital of £230,000 and the usual borrowing powers. The railway had now all the powers necessary to commence building, but construction did not begin for another *eight* years; this delay must have been influenced by the prevailing financial situation evident in the country at that time. In 1866 the bubble had burst on the last of the country's railway manias. The railway investment fever had started early in the decade, people and companies speculated their life savings and investments in fanciful railway schemes, in the hope of 'getting rich quick'. But like previous manias these speculative ventures were to come to nothing, leaving the investors destitute and bankrupt, after the collapse of such eminent merchant bankers as Overend, Gurney & Co. The outcome of these exploits was one of the worst financial crashes of the century. Subsequently it became obvious that some source of Government intervention would be needed to prevent a recurrence of these events. This led to the Railway Companies Act of 1867 which imposed stricter financial control and as a result tightened the reins on railway promoting.

The first Board of Directors (who were also the original promoters - *see page 22*) had, by 1875, completely changed. The new five-man Board was led by the Chairman, William Hawes, Esq., FGS, who was also a trustee of the company. He was no newcomer to the business of railway promoting as he was also the Chairman of the East London Railway which was incorporated in 1865 to take over and convert a tunnel that ran under the River Thames between Rotherhithe and Wapping. There were several similarities between the East London Railway and the Wye Valley Railway; for example neither company ever owned locomotives or rolling stock and both companies had boardroom difficulties. It was also true to say that neither company prospered and both formed what could be called a useful north-south connection.

The second railway personality on the Board was Lord Alexander Gordon Lennox. He would have already experienced Hawes' boardroom manner as he was also a Director of the London, Brighton and South Coast Railway which worked and operated Hawes' East London Railway. The three remaining Directors were Hew Dalrymple, Esq., Trustee of the WVR and Director of the Bristol Port and Channel Dock Co., Clifton; Isaac W. Home, Esq., Director of the Bridgefield and Victoria Co. Ltd., London; and finally James Goodson, Esq., who was the third trustee and also Chairman of the Guardian Fire and Life Assurance Co.

It will be noted that a local connection did not exist between the Board of Directors and the WVR as was common with many other country branches. The Board members were purely business entrepreneurs led by the Chairman, Mr Hawes, who had seen an opportunity to make money by speculating on a railway that for the most part would operate as a north-south link line. It would eventually carry Severn Tunnel traffic north, through Ross, Hereford, Shrewsbury, Chester and on to Manchester and Liverpool, by-passing the congested Midlands. The operating company, the Great Western Railway (GWR) could, except for a short stretch of 50 miles between Hereford & Shrewsbury, use its own company metals. The section between Shrewsbury and Hereford was owned by the Shrewsbury & Hereford Railway and operated jointly by the London & North Western Railway Company and the Great Western Railway.

According to the *Engineering Journal* of June 1874 construction on the Wye Valley project began at Tintern in the second week of May of that year. The contractors, Messrs Reed Bros & Co. of London, took 2½ years to complete just over 13 miles of railway from the Wye Valley Junction to Wyesham, and on Wednesday 1st November, 1876 the line was officially opened to the public.

In January 1877 S.H. Yockney & Son, Engineers, were authorized to sell the locomotive used in the construction of the line and other associated plant; the locomotive appears to have been a Kitson 2-4-0. It was purchased by a company named Lucas & Aird on 1st March, 1877 for the princely sum of £750. A charge of £16 was made for its transportation.

As already mentioned, construction of the line began at Tintern and the civil engineering could be split roughly into two halves, the relatively easy section north of Tintern and the much more difficult southern portion from Tintern to the Wye Valley Junction. The line south from Wyesham to Redbrook was relatively straightforward as regards civil engineering as there were no viaducts, tunnels or vast earthworks to be undertaken. The task involved cutting a shelf along the hillside and building a secure base wide enough for a single track railway; this was achieved by using large pieces of stone to form a stable base for the ballast to lie on, this stone also provided ideal hillside drainage. Large stone blocks can still be seen alongside the track bed between Wyesham and Tintern. A steadily decreasing incline is apparent as the construction work nears Redbrook. Here a bridge and viaduct had to be built, the bridge was to carry the line over a road (now the A466) and the viaduct, a much more splendid affair, to carry the railway over the River Wye to Penallt.

Tintern Abbey and the south end of Tintern tunnel. *The Illustrated London News*

Redbrook station and Penallt viaduct. *The Illustrated London News*

The viaduct was built on a gentle curve and had an overall span of just over 300 feet, it was of iron girder construction supported by four pairs of cast-iron columns. Moving south again from Penallt to Brockweir the engineering involved on this part of the route was very light as the railway followed close to the river on the flat valley floor. Cconstruction work consisted solely of providing a sound track bed that was adequately drained. The drainage arches can still be seen intact between Penallt and Whitebrook. These arches were necessary to allow passage of natural springs and streams beneath the trackbed. From Brockweir to Tintern the line begins to climb away from the river on an incline of 1 in 80 rising steadily to a height of 60 feet at the river bank just south of Tintern station, where the line finished in a vertical drop in the form of a stone parapet. This embankment was needed in order to bring the track level up to the same height as that of the land on the opposite east bank of the Wye, where the railway re-crossed the river via a single span iron bridge having a length of 207 feet (the centre section was removed in the late 1960s).

The bridge was supported by tubular pillars and two stone buttresses, one on each bank, the larger on the east bank is built into the near vertical sides of a tongue of land that juts out into the river. It is here at Tintern that the first and the shorter of the two tunnels on the line was built. It constitutes what would be taken for the Tintern village by-pass, for it was bored through a peninsula of land that is situated directly opposite the village. The tunnel is 182 yards long and was cut through carboniferous limestone, the northern portal being situated directly beneath the monks' path that led from Tintern Abbey to the Malthouse at Brockweir.

From the outset the planning, surveying and civil engineering of the southern portion, the Shorn Cliff section of track between Tintern and Tidenham, was to prove extremely difficult. This was due to the unfavourable topography, which consisted of steep gradients that drew the land towards the river as it neared the estuary. To add to this difficult terrain the steep slopes were covered with dense undergrowth, which made the construction work all the more difficult.

The plan for the Shorn Cliff section was to cut a shelf in the hillside between the two tunnels, Tintern and Tidenham, wide enough for a single track railway and then support the earthwork each side of the line with stone walls, below track level on the riverside and above on the land side, therefore preventing the danger of landslips. These walls, now much overgrown, still remain intact.

The Engineer's plan called for a viaduct to be built along the Shorn Cliff section; this structure was named Black Morgan viaduct, situated a quarter of a mile south of Wireworks Junction. The structure has an overall span of 140 ft and is supported by three semi-eliptical arches.

Immediately south of Black Morgan viaduct the steep gradient of the hillside begins to ease, making construction work less difficult. It is along this section that a stone drainage arch was built with a span of 15 ft, to permit access to the river for a small stream and, nowadays, shelter for a local herd of cattle.

The easy gradient is only evident for a short distance, a quarter of a mile or so north of Tintern Quarry, before the geography takes a turn for the worse, as far as railway engineering is concerned, for here a massive rock face comes into sight and the entrance of the second tunnel. The northern portal marks the place where the railway crosses the ancient fortification of Offa's Dyke.

Without doubt, the most difficult and physically enduring work on the line, took place here, with the boring of the Tidenham or Denhill tunnel as it is sometimes referred to. Here great quantities of material had to be moved, proving to be a formidable task and consuming the greater part of the budget. The boring took two years to complete and was grossly underestimated in cost and length, being 1,188 yards long on completion, compared with the original estimate of 715 yards, making it eventually the 21st longest tunnel on the GWR.

The tunnel was cut through a land mass consisting mainly of limestone, which rose nearly 750 feet from the River Wye below, and it faces a well known landmark in the lower region of the Wye Valley called the Wynd Cliff. Messrs Reed Bros recorded for that time a remarkable rate of progress with the boring, their 'navvies' managing to bore just under six feet a day, a monumental task considering that the workmen had to shift large amounts of earth and rock the hard way by muscle, pick and shovel as mechanical aids were few and rudimentary. On completion, the boring of the tunnel had taken just under 20 months to complete.

South of Tidenham tunnel the construction work was much easier and, to prevent unnecessary gradients, a shallow cutting was excavated starting at the southern portal of the tunnel and finishing just prior to Tidenham station, a distance of just under ¾ mile. The bridge immediately south of Tidenham station was built to carry the line over the A48, the main Chepstow to Gloucester Road, this originally wooden-sided bridge has one iron span supported by two stone-built parapets. The structure underwent a major overhaul in 1978 during which parts of the centre span was strengthened and the wooden sides were replaced with metal sections. The bridge also marks the start of a long, high embankment that carries the railway for ¾ mile, gradually turning west on a steadily decreasing incline of 1 in 66, finishing at the Wye Valley Junction giving access to the South Wales-Gloucester main line and consequently Chepstow via Brunel's magnificent Wye Bridge.

On completion the line had cost a little over £318,000, the largest part of the budget being spent on the construction of Tidenham tunnel.

430.—WYE VALLEY.

Incorporated by 29 and 30 Vic., cap. 357 (10th August, 1866), to construct railways from the South Wales to the Coleford Monmouth Usk and Pontypool and to the South Wales and Great Western Direct. Length. 15 miles. Capital, 230,000*l.* in 20*l.* shares, and 76,600*l.* on loan. Arrangements with Great Western and South Wales and Great Western Direct.

No. of Directors—**5**; minimum, 3; quorum, 3 and 2. *Qualification,* 500*l.*

DIRECTORS :

Jasper Wilson Johns, Esq., Wolverton Park, Newbury, Hants.
Osmond A. Wyatt, Esq., Troy House, Monmouth.

James Murphy, Esq.
Joseph Cary, Esq., 49, Pall Mall, S.W.
Capt. Robert O'Brien Jameson, 60, St. James's Street, Piccadilly, S.W.

Extract from *Bradshaw's Railway Manual* of 1869 and 1870.

Chapter Four

Struggle and Take Over

It was stated on the original Prospectus of 1874 that the line from Monmouth to Tintern was to be completed by the 25th March of that year and the rest by 31st December, 1875. Immediately upon completion, the line was to be taken over by the GWR as the operating company. This was exceeded by several months, the line being finally completed by the Autumn of 1876.

The formal opening day was a grand affair in true Victorian style, in attendance were the Directors and Engineers of the Wye Valley Railway and the officials of the GWR. The special train left Chepstow just after mid-day on 19th October, 1876. The first stop was Tintern, where an invitation to visit the abbey had been extended by His Grace the Duke of Beaufort, lunch was later served in the grounds of the Beaufort Arms.

The party was then taken on to Monmouth where a cordial reception was awaiting them. Bells were ringing and the whole town had turned out to see the special train arrive. The corporation led by the Mayor were assembled on Monmouth Troy station, waiting to greet the visitors and conduct them through the town and the crowds of cheering people to the Beaufort Arms Hotel, where speeches were made and toasts were drunk to celebrate the occasion. For the party's return journey, Tintern Abbey, Tidenham tunnel and the cliffs along the valley were lit with changing coloured lights. Unfortunately this happy note on which the railway began was not to continue. For 29 years the WVR battled for its very existence.

The railway was worked and leased in perpetuity by the GWR, upon the terms of the GWR paying for the first five years a rent of 55 per cent of gross receipts, and after that period 50 per cent of gross receipts. One important advantage which accrued to the WVR from the agreement with the GWR was that its revenue would not be affected in any way by the cost of working expenses, as the WVR would be entitled under all circumstances to receive the above mentioned fixed proportion of the gross receipts, whatever the cost of working the line. This agreement would seem to have been ideal to the WVR. But as the extracts (on page 29) taken from reports of shareholders' meetings dated 1876-1904 show, the company repeatedly made financial losses and continued on a shoe-string existence. The losses were credited to various factors, for example, bad weather, which had a detrimental effect on the much valued tourist trade, the running down and eventual closure of many of the manufacturing industries of the lower Wye Valley, and to a lesser extent, the continuous squabbles and disagreements that were a prominent feature between the owning company and the operating company. This inevitably led to poor services and lack of maintenance, turning the much needed public support against the railway. Lastly and undoubtedly the greatest cross the WVR had to bear was the unprofitable Tintern Railway or Wireworks branch (see Chapter Nine).

All these factors proved too great for the WVR Board of Directors, which itself had experienced problems, arising from mismanagement of company affairs and

GREAT WESTERN RAILWAY.

SUMMER EXCURSIONS

TO

TINTERN

Via THE WYE VALLEY RAILWAY,
AT REDUCED FARES,

From JUNE 4th until further Notice.

From Bristol, Lawrence Hill, Stapleton Road, Clifton Down, and Montpelier	On Mondays and Saturdays.
„ Bath	On Tuesdays and Wednesdays.
„ Cheltenham, Cirencester & Stroud	On Tuesdays.
„ Newport and Gloucester... ...	On Thursdays.
„ Cardiff	On Wednesdays.
„ Hereford	
„ Ross	On Mondays and Thursdays.

TIMES AND FARES.

			First Class.	Second Class.	Third Class.	Return Train from Tintern.
	a.m.	a.m.	s. d.	s. d.	s. d.	
From Bristol	7 15	9 45				4 27 or 7 35 p.m.
„ Lawrence Hill	7 20	9 50				4 27 or 7 35 p.m.
„ Stapleton Road	7 25	9 55	5 0	3 6	2 6	4 27 or 7 35 p.m.
„ Clifton Down...	7 0	9 30				4 27 p.m.
„ Montpelier ...	7 3	9 33				4 27 p.m.
„ Bath	6 35	8 35	6 0	4 6	3 0	4 27 or 7 35 p.m.
„ Cheltenham ...	8 45		7 0	5 0	3 6	4 27 or 7 35 p.m.
		p.m.				
„ Newport	10 40	1 25	5 0	3 6	2 6	4 27 or 7 35 p.m.
„ Cardiff	10 15	12 50	6 0	4 6	3 0	4 27 or 7 35 p.m.
		a.m.				
„ Hereford	6 20	11 0	6 0	4 6	3 0	5 50 p.m.
„ Ross	8 35	11 45	5 0	3 6	2 6	5 50 p.m.
„ Gloucester......	9 15		6 0	4 6	3 0	4 27 or 7 35 p.m.
„ Cirencester ...	7 50		8 0	6 0	4 0	4 27 p.m.
„ Stroud	8 40		7 0	5 0	3 6	4 27 or 7 35 p.m.

Clifton Down and Montpelier Passengers change into the South Wales Union Trains at Stapleton Road. The last Return Train by which there is any connection to Clifton Down or Montpelier leaves Tintern at 4.27 p.m., but Passengers may, if they like, return to Stapleton Road by the Train leaving Tintern at 7.35 p.m.

NOTE.—The 7.15 a.m. Train from Bristol does not run beyond Chepstow, but Passengers are booked through to Tintern by that Train to enable them to visit Chepstow, and they can proceed to Tintern by the 11.22 a.m. Train from Chepstow.

The Tickets are only available on the day of issue, and by the specified Trains, and are not transferable. **Passengers passing through Chepstow may stop there either going or returning.**

J. GRIERSON,

PADDINGTON, *May*, 1879.

GENERAL MANAGER.

Waterlow & Sons Limited, Printers, London Wall, London.

Summer Excursions 1879.

certain irregularities with company funds. In March 1881 these irregularities led to legal action being taken against the Chairman, Mr W. Hawes and other members of the Board, yet another blow to the ill-fated railway.

The Wye Valley Railway's five working years from 1876-1881 under Hawes' control had gone from bad to worse and culminated in the shareholders appointing a Receiver, a Mr Edwin Waterhouse, to sort out the company's ailing affairs. The first move was to appoint a new Chairman and Board of Directors. The new appointments were made, Messrs A. Jerrard (Chairman), F.W. Raikes, E. Toovey and B. Joyner. This time it was also decided on the inclusion of a fifth Board member. The Revd William Dyke was invited to join the Board and he accepted the appointment. Perhaps the idea of a man of God overseeing the affairs of the railway would prevent a recurrence of past events.

The new Board set about their task with fervour but unfortunately the railway was unable to recover and build itself a firm financial base. The WVR finally collapsed towards the closing months of 1889 and for the second time in its short, erratic history a Receiver was appointed, this time to wind up the railway's affairs and to handle the eventual amalgamation with the GWR.

Proposals for the sale of the railway were first started with the GWR in the closing months of 1887. Terms for the amalgamation were agreed upon by both companies and everything would have gone ahead smoothly, but for the intervention of Mr Read, a newly appointed Director to the WVR Board. He stopped the proceedings by sending letters to the shareholders telling them to buy their own shares and not to agree to the sale of the railway. This last initiative was short-lived as the remaining Directors resigned a few months later.

In December 1904 WVR shareholders received a circular from their then Chairman, J.H. Whadcoat, informing them, yet again, of the deteriorating state of the company. The letter went on to explain the negotiations that were taking

Wye Valley Railway trespass notice, sited just north of Tidenham station. *E. Wilmhurst*

WYE VALLEY RAILWAY. Single Line.

Down Trains.

Distance from Monmouth (Troy) Mls. Chs.	STATIONS.	1 Coleford Passenger. arr.	dep.	2 Passenger. arr.	dep.	3 Coleford Passenger. arr.	dep.	4 Passenger. arr.	dep.	Coleford Mixed Train. dep.	6 Goods. arr.	dep.	7 Passenger. arr.	dep.	8 Coleford Mix. Train. arr.	dep.	9 Passenger. arr.	dep.
		A.M.	A.M.	A.M.	A.M.	A.M.	A.M.	P.M.	P.M.	P.M.	P.M.	P.M.	P.M.	P.M.	P.M.	P.M.	P.M.	P.M.
0 61	Monmouth (Troy) Wyesham Junc.	—	8 7	8 50			9 20		12 35	12 50	1 15			4 0				6 10
2 22	Redbrook			9 15	9 16		9 30	12 41	12 42		1 30	1 45	4 4	4 6			6 13	6 16
5 67	Bigswear				9 23			12 49	12 50		2 0	2 10		4 14				6 24
7 12	Tintern			9 29	9 30			12 58	1 0		2 0	2 20	4 23	4 25			6 33	6 35
9 12	Wire Works Junc.				9 31				1 11		C R							
9 77	Tidenham			9 39	9 41			1 9			3 35	3 45	4 34	4 36			6 44	6 46
13 67	Wye Valley Junc.							1 17						4 42				6 52
14 44	Chepstow			9 47	9 50			1 17	1 20		3 55		4 42	4 45			6 52	6 55
19 8	Portskewett			9 58				1 30					4 53				7 5	

▲ This Train will be bunked to Wyesham Junction when necessary, but the load must not exceed 36 Wagons.

Up Trains.

Distance from Portskewett Mls. Chs.	STATIONS.	1 Passenger. arr.	dep.	2 Coleford Passenger. arr.	dep.	3 Goods. arr.	dep.	4 Passenger. arr.	dep.	5 Coleford Passenger. arr.	dep.	6 Coleford Mix. Train. arr.	dep.	7 Passenger. arr.	dep.	8 Coleford Passenger. arr.	dep.	9 Passenger. arr.	dep.
		A.M.	A.M.	A.M.	A.M.	A.M.	A.M.	A.M.	A.M.	P.M.	P.M.	P.M.	P.M.	P.M.	P.M.	P.M.	P.M.	P.M.	P.M.
4 44	Portskewett	—	7 5				10 15	10 55	11 7					2 20	2 35				5 25
6 11	Chepstow	7 15	7 17					11 5	11 7					2 30	2 35			5 30	5 31
6 21	Wye Valley Junc.					10 22	10 30		11 12					2 40	2 41				
9 43	Tidenham	7 22	7 23					11 12	11 13									5 41	5 43
9 76	Wire Works Junc.					10 50	11 33	11 23	11 25					2 51	2 53				
13 21	Tintern	7 33	7 35			11 45	11 50	11 33						3 10	3 12			5 50	5 52
16 66	Bigswear	7 43	7 44			12 5	12 25	11 42	11 44									6 0	6 2
18 27	Redbrook	7 52	7 54		8 57	12 30	12 55	11 50			12 7		2 45	3 18		5 55		6 8	
19 8	Wyesham Junc. Monmouth (Troy)	8 0		9 0		1 0		11 50		12 10									

NO SUNDAY TRAINS.

CROSSING ARRANGEMENTS.

Wyesham Junction and Tintern are the only intermediate Crossing Stations.

No. 4 Up Passenger to pass No. 3 Up Goods at Tintern.

No. 3 Up Goods to cross Nos. 4 and 5 Passenger Trains at Wyesham Junction.

No. 6 Down Goods to cross No. 7 Up Passenger at Tintern.

The Single Line between Monmouth (Troy) and Wye Valley Junction, is worked by Train Staff and Auxiliary Block Telegraph.

Three Train Staffs are in use as under:—

BETWEEN WYE VALLEY JUNCTION AND TINTERN.
Form of Staff and Tickets round—colour white.

BETWEEN TINTERN AND WYESHAM JUNCTION.
Form of Staff and Tickets square—colour yellow.

BETWEEN MONMOUTH (TROY) AND WYESHAM JUNCTION.
Form of Staff and Tickets triangular—colour green.

SPECIAL NOTICES.—All Down Trains proceeding towards Chepstow must stop dead at Tidenham for "Line Clear."

Goods Trains must also stop at the south end of Tidenham Tunnel, when required, to pin down Breaks. Goods Trains proceeding to Monmouth must stop at Wyesham Junction, when required, to pin down Breaks.

Working Timetable for March 1884.

DOWN TRAINS

STATIONS		1 First Coleford Passenger	2 First Birmingham Excursion	3 Second Birmingham Excursion	4 Third Birmingham Excursion	5 Fourth Birmingham Excursion	6 Ordinary Passenger	7 Coleford Passenger	8 Wolverh'pton Excursion	9 Engine of First Birmingham Excursion	10 Ordinary Passenger	11 Coleford Passenger	12 Special Passenger	13 Ordinary Passenger	14 Coleford Passenger	15 Ordinary Passenger	16 Ordinary Passenger
		a.m.	a.m.	a.m.	a.m.	a.m.	a.m.	a.m.	a.m.	p.m.	p.m.	p.m.	p.m.	p.m.	p.m.	p.m.	p.m.
Monmouth	dep	8.3	8.5	8.15	8.29	8.44	9.0	9.20	9.26		12.25	12.50		3.43	4.45	6.0	7.40
Wyesham Junction	"	8.6	8.8	8.18	8.32	8.47	9.3	9.23	9.29		12.27	12.55		3.48	4.50	6.7	7.50
Redbrook	"						9.7				12.31			3.52		6.15	7.53
Bigsweir	"						9.15				12.38			4.0		6.23	7.57
Tintern	arr		8.28	8.38	8.52	9.7	9.25		9.49	12.5	12.45		4.0	4.8		6.26	
	dep			8.43	8.55	9.10	9.35		9.55		12.47		4.4	4.10		6.37	
Tidenham	"			8.58	9.10	9.25	9.38		10.10	12.14	12.56		4.11	4.21		6.40	
Wye Valley Junction	arr			9.03	9.15	9.33	9.40		10.15	12.17	12.59		4.14	4.24		6.43	7.56
Chepstow	dep			9.06	9.18	9.35	9.42		10.18	12.20	1.2		4.17	4.27		6.45	
	arr					9.45	9.51		10.20		1.3		4.20	4.30		6.55	8.07
Portskewett	dep								10.30		1.13		4.30	4.40		7.0	
Severn Tunnel Junction	arr						9.56				1.18		4.35	4.45			8.12

UP TRAINS

STATIONS		1 Ordinary Passenger	2 Coleford Passenger	3 Ordinary Passenger	4 Coleford Passenger	5 Engine of First Birmingham Excursion	6 Coleford Passenger	7 Ordinary Passenger	8 Coleford Passenger	9 Ordinary Passenger	10 First Return Birmingham Excursion	11 Ordinary Passenger	12 Second Return Birmingham Excursion	13 Third Return Birmingham Excursion	14 Fourth Return Birmingham Excursion	15 Return Wolverh'pton Excursion	16 Excursion
		a.m.	a.m.	a.m.	p.m.	p.m.	p.m.	p.m.	p.	p.m.	p.m.	p.m.	p.m.	p.	p.m. r.r.	p.m.	
Severn Tunnel Junction	dep	7.05		10.30		12.55		2.30		5.45	6.20	7.0	7.50		7.55	8.25	
Portskewett	"	7.18		10.36		1.0		2.36		5.51	6.35	7.6	7.54		8.05	8.35	
Chepstow	"	7.19		10.45				2.45		6.0	6.50	7.15	8.10	8.0	8.15	8.45	
	dep	7.22		11.05				2.47		6.6	6.53	7.18	8.15	8.3	8.18	8.48	
Wye Valley Junction	dep			11.08				2.50		6.9		7.21					
Tidenham Junction	"			11.11		1.3		2.53		6.19	7.15	7.25		8.23	8.38	9.08	
Tintern	arr	7.34	8.47	11.21	12.07	1.13	2.30	3.3	5.47	6.24	7.25	7.33	8.32	8.28	8.43	9.13	
	dep	7.36	8.50	11.23	12.10		2.35	3.14	5.50	6.33	7.47		8.35	8.47	9.02	9.32	
Bigsweir	"			11.31				3.24		6.44							
Redbrook	"	7.53		11.41				3.27		6.47	7.50			8.50	9.05	9.35	
Wyesham Junction	"	7.56		11.44				3.30		6.50							
Monmouth	arr	7.58		11.47													

r.r. There trains will run if required only.

CROSSING ARRANGEMENTS No. 10 down train to cross No. 5 up train at W.V. Jct. No. 15 down train to cross No. 9 up train at Tintern. No. 10 down train to cross No. 12 up train at W.V. Jct.

Special timetable of the Wye Valley Railway, Whit Monday, 10th June (assumed date 1889).

The Wye Valley Railway at Llandogo, as it curves round a bend of the river. Two trows are moored on the east bank.   *Monmouth Museum*

Monmouth Troy station *c.* 1900. Mr R. Gooding was the station master at that time.
                                                                                        Monmouth Museum

place with the GWR. In monetary terms the GWR was offering £12 10s. 0d. for each £100 preference stock and 10s. for each £20 ordinary share. The GWR offer was unanimously accepted by the Wye Valley shareholders.

The following summarised extracts from Directors' annual reports to shareholders from 1877-1904 tell some of the story:

28th March, 1879: The receipts continue to improve. Passengers carried in last six months have been 54,234 against 38,555 in the six months ending 30th June, 1878. An increase of 40 per cent and the goods 14,640 tons against 11,373 an increase of 28 per cent. The gross receipts for the half year have been £2,836 14s. 1d. against £2,098 19s. 4d. for the half-year ending 30th June, 1878 an increase of 35 per cent.

11th September, 1879: Receipts down to £1,975 4s. 11d. Most unsatisfactory. But due to wetness of season and depression of trade.

March 1881: Wireworks branch constructed at needless expense. Thought by Directors a source of considerable gain as much traffic uses line. However, company have no power to receive tolls in respect of branch. So have no funds for its maintenance but trust that GWR will see advantage to them of keeping it open.

September 1881: Lost money again (£53 18s. 1d.) caused by diversion of traffic from Bristol over Severn Bridge after pier at Portskewett had been burned. Company offered wharves but GWR declined (prejudicial to company).

March 1882: Receipts still falling. Causing anxiety but not without hope. GWR still being awkward - refusing facilities for passenger traffic etc.

December 1882: Increase of over £500: would have been more but Redbrook tinplate works closed. GWR being more liberal - residents of locality sent petition to GWR for improved services.

December 1883: Still losing money, negotiations with Golden Valley Railway Company for running powers over line, but GV Co., not yet applied for Parliamentary powers.

December 1904: Letters sent to shareholders stating terms of GWR. Each £100 Wye Valley Railway 5 per cent debenture stock to be exchanged for equal amounts of GWR 4½ per cent stock. £12 10s. 0d. in cash to be given for each £100 of WVR preference stock. 10s. per share for each WVR ordinary share. Payment of £600 to discharge liabilities. WVR now indebted to GWR about £30,000.

A wonderfully evocative scene at Tintern in the early years of the 20th century.
Lens of Sutton

A busy scene at Tintern station in 1906.   *Provenance Unknown*

A view of Tintern Abbey from the trackbed of the Wye Valley Railway.   *B.M. Handley*

Chapter Five

Decline and Closure

Total amalgamation with the GWR was completed by 1st July, 1905, and as far as the travelling public was concerned the relinquishing of power by the WVR was a good thing. As now the railway came under control of the GWR, improved services were soon evident and maintenance that had fallen behind was rectified. The service became fairly consistent throughout the year with four or five trains a day in each direction, operating on a Monday to Saturday timetable. (This service was complemented by additional trains introduced after 1918. This was a summer Sunday service to take advantage of the weekend tourists to this world famous beauty spot. The excursions were operated consistently up to the early part of 1939 when they were finally dropped due to the outbreak of war.)

The most popular trains during the line's history were those organized as special excursions to see Tintern Abbey on the night of the harvest moon. Each September crowds of between 1,000 and 1,300 people came by train from Gloucester, Cheltenham, Newport and Cardiff to glimpse the full moon shining through the abbey's rose window. In the 1950s the quiet routine of the railway was interrupted by the rare excitement of a twice-yearly double-headed, seven-coach excursion from London, this certainly enlivened the serenity of a peaceful Monmouth Sunday afternoon.

While under GWR control other alterations gradually took place to improve the service to the local community, new halts being opened to complement the four rather widespread original stations. The halts added in chronological order were Whitebrook, Llandogo, Brockweir, Wyesham, Penallt and finally Netherhope. Special instructions were issued for the working of trains along the branch. The following is an extract from a special instruction issued to station masters and guards and dated June 1889.

Trains not exceeding 7 vehicles - Rear vehicles to be braked, a guard to ride in it.
Trains comprising 8 to 14 vehicles - Front and rear vehicles to be brakes, a guard to ride in each.
Trains comprising 15 to 20 vehicles - Front and rear vehicles and vehicle in centre of train to be brakes and a guard to ride in each.

The greatest movement of traffic on the branch took place during the summer months which made the signalman's job a busy one, owing to the fact that the branch was single line throughout its entire length, with the exception of a few passing loops. From the Wye Valley Junction to Wyesham the line was divided into six sections.

Like many rural services across the country, the Wye Valley line suffered gradual losses in revenue during the inter-war period (1918-1939). There were several reasons for this decline in the railway's popularity. The most immediate and obvious was the gradual improvement that was taking place in the roads and the steady rise in the use of motor transport. The internal combustion engine began to pressurise the railways at a local and national level on three

WYE VALLEY RAILWAY.   Single Line.   (No Sunday Trains.)

DOWN TRAINS.

Distance from Monmouth M.C.	Station No.	Gradient 1 in	Point to Point Times. Mins.	Allow for Stop. Mins.	Allow for Start. Mins.	STATIONS.	1 B Coleford Pass. dep. A.M.	2 B Passenger arr. A.M.	dep. A.M.	8 B Coleford Pass. dep. A.M.	Goods S.T. 523 arr. A.M.	dep. A.M.	4 Passenger arr. P.M.	dep. A.M.	Coleford Mixed Train arr. P.M.	dep. P.M.	6 Goods S.T. 522 arr. P.M.	dep. P.M.	7 Passenger arr. P.M.	dep. P.M.	8 Coleford Mixed Train arr. P.M.	dep. P.M.	9 Passenger arr. P.M.	dep. P.M.	10 Passenger arr. P.M.	dep. P.M.
0 61	2631	—	—	—	—	Monmouth (Troy)	7 52	8 40		9 40				12 17	12 55		1 15		4 0		4 25		5 57		
2 21	2633	66 R	3	1	1	Wyesham Junct.	8	8 59		9 43			12 10		1 0		1 30			4 2	4 50		6 39			
3 60	2634	80 F	4	1	1	Redbrook			9 9					12 23			2 25		4 6				6 3		6 11
5 9	2635	132 F	8	1	1	St. Briavels & Llandogo		9 17	9 18					12 31			2 10		4 14			6 17	6 11		6 21
6 17	2636	80 R	8	1	1	Tintern (for Brockweir)							X12 38	X12 38		2 35		4 20	4 23			6 21		
9 5	2637	80 F				Wire Works Junction			9 27																
12 79	2638	66 F	15	1		Tidenham		9 32	9 37				12 50	12 47			3 45	3 40		4 31	4 34		6 29	6 31		
13 64	2649	66 F	3	1		Wye Valley Junction		9 46					12 52	1 28			3 55		4 39	4 42		X	6 37		
14 47	2650	—	—			Chepstow								1 37				C R		4 51			6 34		6 46
19 9	2651	—	—			Portskewett																			
21 73	2655	—	—			Severn Tunnel Junc.		9 52					1 42				6 25		4 57			6 52			

UP TRAINS.

Distance from Severn Tunnel Junc. M.C.	Gradient 1 in	Point to Point Times. Mins.	Allow for Stop. Mins.	Allow for Start. Mins.	STATIONS.	B Passenger arr. A.M.	dep. A.M.	2 B Coleford Pass. arr. A.M.	3 B Coleford Pass. arr. A.M.	Goods S.T. 523 arr. A.M.	dep. A.M.	4 Passenger arr. A.M.	dep. A.M.	5 Passenger arr. A.M.	dep. A.M.	6 Coleford Mixed Train arr. P.M.	dep. P.M.	7 Passenger arr. P.M.	dep. P.M.	8 Coleford Passenger. arr. P.M.	dep. P.M.	Passenger arr. P.M.	dep. P.M.
2 64	—	—	—	—	Severn Tunnel Junc.		6 50			10 45			10 40		11 28	11 36		2 30				6 21	
26	—	—	—	—	Portskewett		7 9			10 50			11 0					2 37				6 28	
8 70	—	—	—	—	Chepstow	7 2	7 11			11 15	11 20	X12 45	X11 0	11 45				2 48				6 38	
8 74	266 R	4	1	1	Wye Valley Junction	7 7	7 16			12 55		11 0	11 28	12 0				2 54				6 44	X
12 24	66 R	11	1	1	Tidenham					X12 0		1 22	12 0									7 10	
12 56	95 F	8	1	1	Tintern (for Brockweir)	7 23	7 25			11 15		X11 46		12 12			3 2	X3 4				6 52	
18 4	80 F	11	1		St. Briavels & Llandogo	7 39	7 32			12 55		11 53					3 11					7 1	
19 52	170 R	10	1		Redbrook		7 41			X12 0		12 0		12 5			3 18	3 20				7 7	
21 12	211 R	6	1	1	Wyesham Junct.	7 39	7 44	8 42	11 63	1 30		12 5		1 22			3 23			5 45		7 13	
21 73	60 R	—	—	—	Monmouth (Troy)	7 46		8 45	11 56	1 35		1 22			11 36	2 42		3 25		5 47		7 15	

Single Line between Monmouth (Troy) and Wye Valley Junction worked by Electric Train Staff.

The intermediate Crossing Stations are **TINTERN** and **WYESHAM JUNCTION**.

W — This Train will be banked to Wyesham Junction when necessary, but the load must not exceed 35 Wagons.

Working Timetable for April 1910.

An aerial view of Tintern. In the centre of the picture is Tintern Abbey, which generated much excursion traffic for the railway. The viaduct which carried the Wireworks branch to Abbey Tinplate Works can be clearly seen (*see Chapter Nine*).

Provenance Unknown

EACH WEEK-DAY

G.W.R. CIRCULAR TOUR FROM GLOUCESTER
THROUGH THE

BEAUTIFUL WYE VALLEY

enabling passengers to visit

Ross-on-Wye, Symonds Yat
Monmouth, Tintern or Chepstow

CHEAP DAY CIRCULAR TOUR TICKETS are issued from GLOUCESTER

RETURN FARE **5/0** THIRD CLASS

Passengers may travel on the forward journey via Ross-on-Wye and Monmouth, returning via Chepstow and Grange Court; or forward via Grange Court and Chepstow, returning via Monmouth and Ross-on-Wye. They may also break their journey at Chepstow, Tintern, St. Briavels, Llandogo, Redbrook-on-Wye, Monmouth, Symonds Yat, or Ross-on-Wye, but must return to Gloucester the same day.

THREE WYE VALLEY Circular Tours by G.W.R. from NEWPORT

RETURN FARES 3rd class

The following is an itinerary of each Tour :—

TOUR No. 1.—Raglan, Monmouth, Tintern, Chepstow. Passengers travel to Tintern either via Chepstow or via Pontypool Road and Monmouth, and are entitled to break the journey either going or returning at Raglan, Monmouth, Redbrook-on-Wye, St. Briavels, Tintern, or Chepstow, and to travel to and fro by either route . **3s. 8d.**

TOUR No. 2.—Usk, Monmouth, Symonds Yat, Chepstow. Passengers travel to Symonds Yat either via Chepstow and Monmouth, or via Pontypool Road and Monmouth, and may break their journey either going or returning at Usk, Raglan, Monmouth, Redbrook-on-Wye, St. Briavels, Tintern or Chepstow, enabling them to travel to or fro by either route . **4s. 6d.**

TOUR No. 3.—Monmouth, Symonds Yat, Ross-on-Wye, Chepstow. Passengers travel to Ross-on-Wye either via Chepstow and Monmouth or via Pontypool Road and Monmouth, and may break their journey either going or returning at Usk, Raglan, Monmouth, Redbrook-on-Wye, St. Briavels, Tintern, Chepstow, Symonds Yat, or Kerne Bridge, enabling them to travel to or fro by either route . **5s. 6d.**

For further details see handbills obtainable at local stations.

G.W.R. CHEAP DAY FARES FOR RAMBLERS.

FROM	To Newport 1st	3rd	To Abergavenny 1st	3rd	To Hereford 1st	3rd	To Ross-on-Wye 1st	3rd	To Symonds Yat 1st	3rd	To M'nm'th Troy 1st	3rd	To M'nm'th May Hill 1st	3rd	To Lydney 1st	3rd	To Usk 1st	3rd	To Tintern 1st	3rd	To Chepstow 1st	3rd	To Gloucester 1st	3rd	To Pontypool Rd. 1st	3rd	To Raglan 1st	3rd
ABERDARE(high l)	5 1½	3 11½	6 3	4 2	2 11	2 7	5	—	—	—	—	—	—	—	—	—	—	—	—	—	—	—	—	—	4 9	3 2	—	—
ABERGAVENNY	4 0	2 8	—	—	4 9	3 2	7	2 4	9 6	3 4	2 5	2 3	5 2	8 1	9	—	—	—	—	—	—	—	—	2 0 1	4 4	0 2	8	—
ABERTILLERY	3 5 2	3	2c 9	1c10	—	—	—	—	7	2 4	9 5	11 3 11	—	—	—	—	7 11 5	3 7	2 4	9	—	—	—	—	—	4 9	3 2	
BLAENAVON	3 0 2	0 3	6 2	4 7	6 5	0 7 11 5	3 6	3 4	2 5	6 3	8 2	9 1 10	—	—	—	—	8	9 1 10	—	—	—	—	—	—	4 0	2 8		
CHELTENHAM(S.J.)	—	—	—	—	7 6 5	0 4 11 3	3 6	9 4	6	—	7 6 5	0 5 6 3	8	—	—	—	7 11 5	3 7	2 4	9	—	—	—	—	—	—	—	—
CHEPSTOW	3 6 2	4	—	—	5 6 3	8 4 5 2 11	3 2 2 1	—	—	—	—	—	—	—	—	1 3	9½	—	—	5 6 3	8	—	—	4 5 2 11				
EBBW VALE	4 5 2 11	—	—	—	7 11 5	3 6	9 4	6	—	—	—	—	—	—	—	8 8 5	9 7 11 5	3	—	—	—	—	5 6 3	8				
GLOUCESTER	—	—	—	—	6 0 4	0 3 6 2	4 5	2 3	5	—	6 0 4	0 4 0 2	8	—	—	—	6 3 4	2 5	6 3	8	—	—	—	—	—	—	—	—
HENGOED(high l.)	—	—	4 5 2 11	9 0 6	0 8 3 5	6 7	2 4	9 5	11 3 11	—	—	—	—	3 6 2	4	—	—	—	—	—	—	—	2 5 1	7 4	9 3	2			
MONMOUTH(Troy)	5 6 3	8 5	2 3 5	5	2 3	3 2	9 1 10	1 3	9½	—	—	2 6 1	8 2	0 1	4 3	0 2	0 6	3 4	2 3	6 2	4 1	5 11						
NEWNHAM	—	—	—	—	2 9 1 10	—	—	—	—	—	2 0 1	4	—	—	—	—	3 6 2	4	—	—	—	—	—	—	—	—	—	—
NEWPORT	—	4 0 2	8 8	5 9	8 3 5	6 6	9 4	6 5	6 3	8	—	—	2 1c1	11 4	9 3	2 3	6 2	4 9	0 6	0 1	8 1	1 4	2 2 9					
PONTYPOOL ROAD	1 8 1	2 0 1	4 6	9 4	6 6	3 4	2 4	9 3	2 3	6 2	4	—	—	1 3	9½	—	—	—	—	—	—	—	2 5 1	7				
RISCA	1 5	11	—	—	—	—	7 11 5	3 7	2 4	9	—	—	5 11 3 11	4 9 3	2	—	—	—	—	—	—	5 2 3	5					
ROSS-ON-WYE	—	—	2 6 1	8	—	—	1	—	1 8	—	—	—	—	—	—	—	—	—	—	—	—	—	—	—	—	—	—	—
STROUD	—	—	8 5 5	7 5	11 3 11	5	0	—	—	—	6 3 4	2	—	—	—	—	8 8 5	9 7 11 5	3	—	—	—	—	—	—	—		

c.—Via Brynmawr and L.M.S. Railway.

The above tickets are issued each weekday (and also on Sundays where train service is available) by any train.

NOTE.—For particulars of further Cheap Day Tickets from other Stations, see handbills and notices obtainable at Stations in the district concerned.

'Ramblers' Return Specials' were introduced by the GWR to promote its country network which ran through some beautiful scenery in England and Wales.

WYE VALLEY JUNCTION
140 M. 50 C.
(via Gloucester)

TIDENHAM
0 M. 70 C.
(from Wye Valley Jcn)

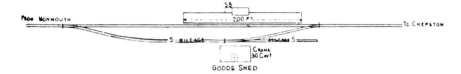

TINTERN for BROCKWEIR
4 M. 52 C.
(from Wye Valley Jcn)

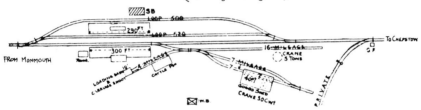

St BRIAVELS and LLANDOGO
8 M. 0 C.
from Wye Valley Jcn

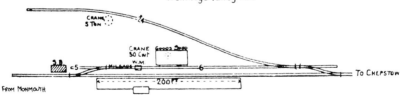

REDBROOK
11 M. 48 C.
(from Wye Valley Jcn)

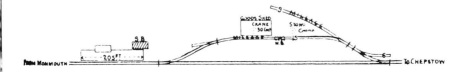

Tintern station, with Ted Wheeler, station master (*centre*) in 1931.   *B. Wakeham*

Pannier tank No. 6417 stands at Tintern station on 22nd August, 1958.   *E. Wilmhurst*

fronts, i.e. lorries (goods traffic), buses (passenger transport), and to a much lesser extent motor cars (private traffic). There were efforts made by the GWR to attract people back to the line by introducing steam railcars and, at a later date, the diesel railcar, a simple and cheap mode of carrying light passenger traffic. But unfortunately the writing was on the wall; even before the publication of the (1963) Beeching Report the line was realised to be uneconomical. It was costing British Railways in excess of £20,000 per annum when the decision was taken to abandon passenger traffic, and it had become obvious that the area was better served by road transport. The last regular passenger train ran on Saturday 3rd January, 1959. For driver Charles Collins, fireman Bill Oak and guard Stanley Forster this must have been a sad day. The line was officially closed to passenger traffic on Monday 5th January, 1959. A report in the following day's newspaper said: 'No more would people be able to enjoy the most beautiful railway journey in Britain'.

The final passenger train to use the branch was an eight-coach special train organised by W.A. Camwell on behalf of the Stephenson Locomotive Society. It was probably the longest train on the line since the heyday of the excursions and was entirely composed of ex-GWR stock, leaving Chepstow at 11.20 am on 4th January, 1959. Two pannier tanks hauled the train, 0-6-0 No. 6412 with driver A. Bowen and fireman J.M. Thomas and No. 6439, whose driver C. Barrett had fireman O.T. Williams beside him on the footplate. Guard Frank Jones was kept busy punching hundreds of tickets, while locomotive inspector T.A. Mountjoy was also travelling to make sure everything went according to plan. Railway pensioners and others connected with the line travelled on the train, augmenting the numbers to some 408. They included a Mr Palmer, farmer at St Briavels, whose father and grandmother travelled on the first train of the Wye Valley Railway, and whose grandfather became a farmer of substance by supplying the local contractors engaged in the extended excavation of Tidenham tunnel, the longest on the line.

After a fine view of the snow-encircled ruins of Tintern Abbey and a glimpse on emerging from Tintern tunnel of a trespass warning board bearing the name 'Wye Valley Railway', the train halted briefly at Tintern station. After passing St Briavels and its crossing box with the only moveable distant signals on the whole line, the next stop was Redbrook-on-Wye separated from the preceding Penallt Halt only by the viaduct over the River Wye.

With a view of the site of the long-abandoned Coleford branch descending steeply from the woods to the east, the approach to Monmouth Troy was heralded uniquely, even for a last train, by a pelting with snowballs from local youths as it passed the housing estate on the outskirts of Monmouth adjoining Wyesham Halt!

Perhaps this unusual sight for a Monmouthshire Sunday could not be endured by local inhabitants, for very few, considering the size of the town, witnessed the final closure to passenger traffic of the last two of Monmouth's one-time four branches.

For nearly 90 years steam locomotives had wound their sinuous course up and down the Wye Valley. Being pulled along in a smartly painted carriage was a leisurely experience evocative of an age when 'time' was considered less

Two dramatic views of a flooded St Briavels station in 1955.   *(Both) Pat Kedward*

The SLS Special at Redbrook station. The train is facing Monmouth, with the River Wye to the right of the picture. *B.M. Handley*

Station staff and train crew with the last freight train at Monmouth Troy on 4th January, 1964. *Left to right*; Eric Broom (fireman) Bill Thomas (driver) Harry 'Duckie' Williams, Chris Deakin, Ernie Williams, Alan Musker, Reg Williams, Harry George (C&W Dept), Mervyn Harris, Phil Williams, Harry Harris, Lou Jenkins, Mrs Wallett and Charlie Hawker.

Arthur Day

important than it is today. On a summer afternoon with the fresh country air blowing through the carriage windows the 14½ mile journey from Monmouth to Chepstow would take 45 to 50 minutes with the train stopping at eight halts and four stations. For the tourist the branch provided superb views of the Wye Valley and its magnificent surrounding countryside.

Had Monmouth remained the county town of Monmouthshire it would have been the first county town ever to have lost its passenger service.

Freight trains continued to operate between Chepstow and Monmouth for five more years after the abolition of the passenger service. Goods and freight services were finally withdrawn in January 1964. Shortly afterwards much of the track was lifted. The continuity of the trackbed was broken with the removal of bridge sections at Wyesham, Redbrook, Tintern and the metal section of the viaduct at Monmouth. The realignment of the A466 road also contributed to trackbed destruction. The trackbed often gets completely overgrown in the summer months and reveals itself again in the cold seasons when the long grass and brambles have died back. Attempts to convert the trackbed to cycle track have (so far) failed except for the section from Wyesham to Redbrook.

If the railway is not to be used again to meet the demand for limestone, surely with the tremendous increase in tourism witnessed today, somebody somewhere must see the potential of re-opening the line again for part of the way. Perhaps passengers on special excursions could travel as far as Tintern where a new station could be constructed on the river bank opposite the abbey. A short walk over a safer Wireworks bridge could take tourists to see the delights of Tintern. Tintern tunnel could house the rolling stock and maybe visiting steam engines from preserved lines.

Until that great day arrives people will have to be content to go back in time and appreciate the outstanding natural beauty of the Wye Valley by simply walking along the established footpaths.

A portrait of, *from left to right*; 'Duckie' Williams, Ernie Watkins, Harry George, Reg Williams and Charlie Hawker as they stand next to the engine on the last freight from Monmouth Troy on 4th January, 1964.   *Arthur Day*

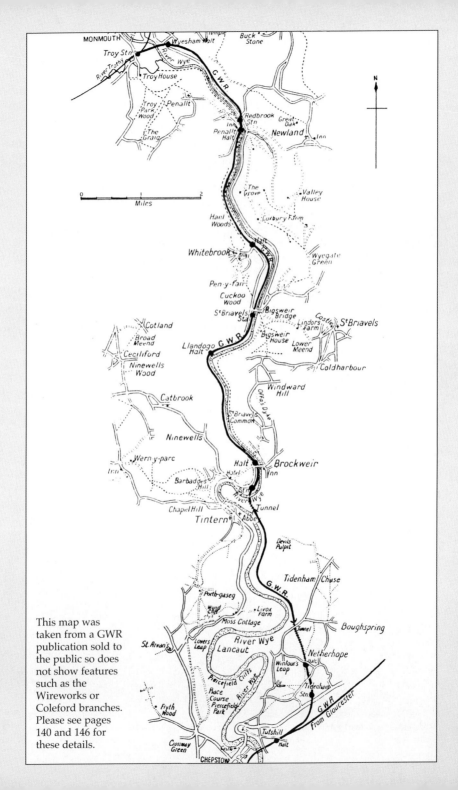

MONMOUTH

Wyesham Halt

Troy Stn

River Trothy

River Wye

Buck Stone

Temple

G W R

Troy House

Troy Park Wood

Penallt

The Graig

Redbrook Stn

Great Oak

Inn
Penallt Halt

Newland

Inn

0   1   2
Miles

The Grove

Valley House

Luxbury F. Stm

Haël Woods

Halt

Whitebrook

Inn

Wyegate Green

Pen-y-fan

Cuckoo Wood

Bigsweir Bridge

St Briavels Stn

Castle

St Briavels

Lindors Farm

G W R

Cotland

Broad Meend

Bigsweir House

Lower Meend

Llandogo Halt

Ceciliford

Ninewells Wood

Coldharbour

Catbrook

Windward Hill

Offa's Dyke

Ninewells

Briavels Common

Wern-y-parc

Inn

Halt

Brockweir

Hotel

Inn

Barbadoes Hill

River Wye

Chapel Hill

Tunnel

Tintern

Abbey

Devils Pulpit

Tidenham Chase

G. W. R

Porth-gaseg

Wynd Cliff

Livox Farm

Boughspring

Moss Cottage

St. Arvan's

Lovers Leap

River Wye
Lancaut

Wintour's Leap

Netherhope

Halt

Tunnel

Piercefield Cliffs

Tidenham Stn

G. W. R

From Gloucester

Race Course
Piercefield Park

River Wye

Flyth Wood

Tutshill

Halt

Cromway Green

CHEPSTOW

This map was
taken from a GWR
publication sold to
the public so does
not show features
such as the
Wireworks or
Coleford branches.
Please see pages
140 and 146 for
these details.

Chapter Six

Signalling, Stations and Halts

Signalling

Signals and signal boxes on the Wye Valley Railway were supplied by McKenzie & Holland of Worcester, the well-known signalling contractors who equipped numerous similar small railways. Boxes were built at Redbrook (10 levers?), Bigsweir, Tintern (25 levers), Tidenham and Wye Valley Jn where the line joined the South Wales main line from Gloucester. The latter box was built of brick, the others on the Wye Valley itself being of stone. When the Coleford branch was built, it was equipped with standard GWR Type 3 boxes at Wyesham Jn, Newland and Coleford.

By 1884 at least, the line was worked by Train Staff & Ticket with telegraph instruments. The sections were: Monmouth Troy to Wyesham Jn - green triangular train staff; Wyesham Jn to Tintern - square yellow train staff; Tintern to Wye Valley Jn - round white train staff.

Though the other stations were then fully signalled, Tintern and Wyesham Jn were the only crossing places on the line. All down trains were to stop dead at Tidenham for 'Line clear' from Wye Valley Jn. At some stage arrangements were made for the telegraph apparatus at Tidenham and Redbrook to be switched through when these places were unmanned.

Though staff and ticket working usually sufficed with the sparse timetable, it was rather inflexible and as part of a programme of improving branch lines, in 1907 the whole line was converted to Electric Train Staff (ETS). The sections then became Monmouth Troy-Wyesham Jn-Redbrook-Bigsweir-Tintern-Tidenham-Wye Valley Jn. In addition to the ETS working, ET Tablet sections were introduced between Wyesham Jn and Bigsweir, and between Tintern and Wye Valley Jn, to enable Redbrook and Tidenham boxes to be closed when not required. Tablet instruments were at this time finding favour on the GWR, the difference between the long metal staff and the round tablet being considered an additional reminder to drivers whether they were working over a long or short section. The new equipment was brought into use on Sunday, 1st December. In connection with the new switching-out apparatus, Tidenham and Bigsweir boxes were both fitted with new lever frames of the GWR stud type, both of 15 levers.

Ground frames existed at Redbrook (South), Tintern Wireworks siding, Tintern Quarry North and South, in each case working adjacent points and facing point locks and being released by a key on the train staff. Tintern Wireworks ground frame, and possibly others, was originally covered.

Following the temporary closure of the Coleford branch as a World War I economy, Wyesham Jn box was closed and boarded up, the section being extended to Monmouth Troy. The signal arms at Wyesham Jn were removed, though the box was not finally abolished until 1927.

Signalling economies now followed thick and fast; Redbrook box was reduced to ground frame status on 11th January, 1927, the staff section being

Green-handled WVR train staff. This is now on display at the GWR Museum at Coleford.
R. Dingwall

extended to Monmouth Troy. Tidenham box closed on 30th October, 1928, to be replaced by open ground frames. Bigsweir (by now known as St Briavels) was reduced to ground frame status on 21st November; here, however, Stop signals were retained in each direction to protect the level crossing. Henceforth the branch was worked as two sections, Monmouth-Tintern-Wye Valley Jn.

At Wye Valley Jn a short length of double line existed, with a catch-point to prevent any vehicles running back on the steep gradient towards Tidenham fouling the main line. In July 1936 the layout was simplified and an ash drag provided instead of the simple catch-point, the portion of double line being singled at the same time.

Following the closure of the line to passengers, St Briavels ground frame closed on 2nd February, 1959. Tintern lingered on until 27th March, 1960, after which the branch was worked as one section from Wye Valley Jn using a wooden train staff. The signal box here remained in use until 3rd March, 1969 when it was closed as part of the scheme to extend the area of control of Newport panel box.

Control of the junction now passed to a 5-lever open ground frame on the up side of the main line. The crossover road having been removed under the scheme, trains from the branch had to run down the up main to the east end of Chepstow where another ground frame worked a crossover between the main lines. Both ground frames were released from Newport panel. The remains of the branch were then worked as a siding.

Stations

Without a doubt, a journey along the Wye Valley Railway from Chepstow to Monmouth Troy was one of the most charming journeys of all our rural branch lines. Where else could one cross the ancient earthworks of Offa's Dyke, marvel at the magnificent forest or the historic ruined splendour of Tintern Abbey, and throughout the enjoyable journey have the companionship of the River Wye, entertained by its rhythmic flow, kept in strict tempo by the mechanical music of the little tank engine.

When the railway first opened for passenger traffic the stations were Redbrook, Bigsweir, Tintern and Tidenham. But as passenger services and trade increased, alterations and additions were made to the initial complement of stations. The stations and halts in this chapter are arranged in chronological order from the southernmost end of the line (Wye Valley Junction) to Monmouth Troy station.

Tidenham

The 1 in 66 climb from Wye Valley Junction culminates on a high embankment that finishes at Tidenham station. The station was opened in November 1876 and is one of four stations built during the construction of the line. The village of Tidenham is mentioned as early as the 10th century when in 956 AD, the year after his coronation, King Edwy, son of Edmund, presented the Royal Manor of Tidenham to the monks of Bath Abbey.

When Tidenham station first opened the complex comprised of a platform and station buildings, signal box and goods shed. The track layout consisted of a loop which ran parallel to the station and a short spur siding that served the goods shed. This arrangement remained for half a century, until the closure of the signal box in the autumn of 1928. Control of the loop and siding was then given over to ground frame levers positioned north and south of the loop. The last major alteration at Tidenham during the railway's working life happened in the winter of 1952 when the loop and consequently the south ground frame were taken out of use. The north frame and goods siding remained until February 1955 when it too was abandoned.

Tidenham station was to gain the unhappy distinction of becoming the first station to close on the line in January 1917, as a wartime measure to release staff. It remained closed for just over a year before it was re-opened on 1st February, 1918 because of 'the traffic in connection with the new shipbuilding yard at Beachley, the crowded state of the accommodation at Chepstow and the handling of additional traffic for the Road Board' [General Manager's monthly report to the Board]. It then remained open until 1959, ending its days having been demoted to the status of a halt.

The station buildings, signal box and goods shed were demolished soon after closure, as the site was taken over by quarry contractors who developed the original platform into a loading bay for locally quarried ballast stone. In March 1968 a new loop (again running parallel to the platform) and two new ground frames were laid so as to provide a run-round for the ballast trains.

Two views of Tidenham station after closure to passengers.   *(Both) Lens of Sutton*

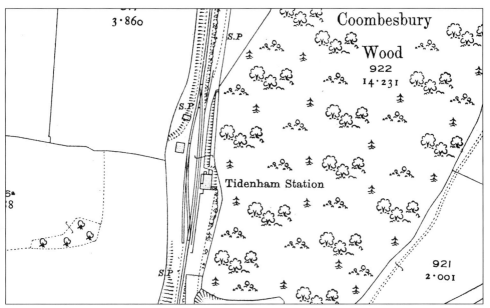

Tidenham station.   *Reproduced from the 25", 1921 Ordnance Survey Map*

Class '37' No. 37231 is seen with an empty ballast train for Tintern Quarry, passing the site of Tidenham station in June 1979. The new loop is shown in the foreground.   *B.M. Handley*

Pannier tank No. 6426 arrives at Netherhope Halt with a train for Chepstow having just emerged from Tidenham tunnel. *B.L. Jenkins*

Plan of the halt shelter used at Netherhope and elsewhere along the line. *B.M. Handley*

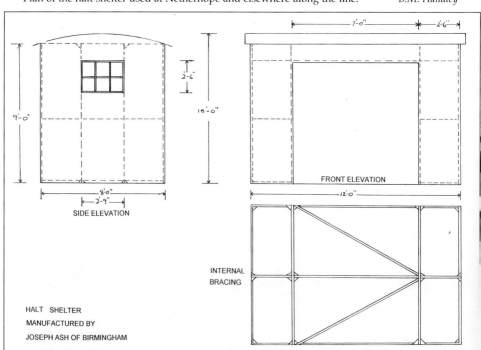

SIDE ELEVATION

FRONT ELEVATION

INTERNAL
BRACING

HALT SHELTER
MANUFACTURED BY
JOSEPH ASH OF BIRMINGHAM

Class '37' No. 37238 emerges from the heavily overgrown southern portal of Tidenham tunnel with a down ballast train in July 1979. Netherhope Halt was situated on the right of the photograph.   *B.M. Handley*

Netherhope Halt

Netherhope was the last halt to be built on the branch. Construction commenced in the spring of 1932 and it was brought into use in July of that year. The halt was situated just south of the southern portal of Tidenham tunnel, and the approach to the platform was down a steep path that led from the road bridge. The galvanised corrugated shelters that were used on the halt sites at Netherhope, Penallt, Brockweir and Llandogo were built and supplied by Joseph Ash & Son Ltd of Birmingham. The company specialised in hot dip galvanised structures which were ideal for long term exposure to the elements. The halt was closed to passengers in January 1959 and demolished soon afterwards. Nothing now remains of the site.

Tintern

Tintern station was the largest railway complex on the branch. It was opened to the travelling public in November 1876. The layout consisted of a main station platform, an island platform, signal box, goods shed, loading bays, cattle pens and several sidings. The station was erected during the initial construction of the line and it was anticipated that Tintern village with its world famous abbey would become a busy tourist attraction. This was partly the reason for the extent of railway development at Tintern, including the doubling of the running lines and the construction of a loop on the down side ('down' was towards Wye Valley Jn), making the down platform an island which could be used for trains starting for Chepstow, but not for Monmouth. Siding signals controlled the exit of trains at either end of the loop; for entrance to the loop there were separate arms on the home signals. The loop experienced many 'Abbey Excursions' during the summer

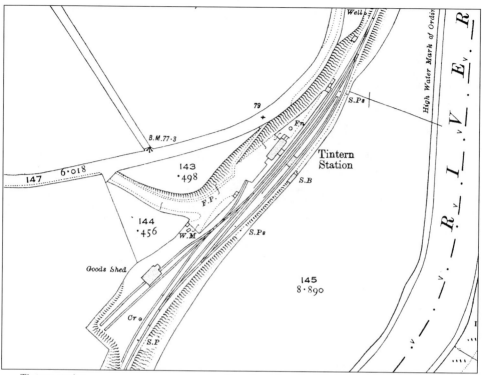

Tintern station.

Reproduced from the 25", 1921 Ordnance Survey Map

Tintern station with milk churns ready for loading onto the next passenger train.

Lens of Sutton

View looking north at Tintern. *Lens of Sutton*

A northbound auto-train is being loaded with boxes and baskets at Tintern. *Lens of Sutton*

Brockweir Halt on 15th October, 1958. Approaching the halt is 0-6-0 pannier tank No. 6426 on the 11.50 am train from Monmouth Troy.   *W.A. Camwell*

'14XX' class 0-4-2T No. 1421 approaches Brockweir Halt with the 11.50 am from Monmouth Troy on 5th March, 1958.   *R.O. Tuck*

months from the late 1870s to the early 1950s. The goods shed loading docks and cattle/sheep pens were situated south of the passenger station. Part of the goods sidings were removed pre-1960, before the final closure of the line in 1964.

The station complex has survived the inevitable deterioration and destruction that normally accompanies closure. This has been due to the action of Gwent County Council Planning Department, with assistance from the Countryside Commission, who have renovated the complex and turned it into a picnic site. Much of the station has been restored and it now houses a permanent exhibition with photographs and artifacts depicting the history of the Wye Valley Railway. The signal box, also renovated, is now office accommodation for the Wye Valley Information Service.

Brockweir Halt

Brockweir village was originally served by Tintern station which was situated some distance from the village. Brockweir eventually gained its own halt in the autumn of 1929, being officially opened to the public on 23rd September, 1929. Nothing now remains of the halt site which was situated at the north side of Brockweir bridge. The railway arch of the bridge is now filled in and it is quite easy to miss the fact that the bridge once spanned the railway as well as the river. Trackbed between the site of Brockweir Halt and 'Catchmans Court' (the large house up river of the Halt on the same side) is now long overgrown and has been buried by the realignment of the A466.

Llandogo Halt

Llandogo Halt was opened to traffic just after Whitebrook Halt in March 1927. Prior to the opening of the halt, Llandogo had been served by St Briavels station, which meant a walk of just over a mile or so for the inhabitants of Llandogo village. So the new halt was welcomed. The halt site was the smallest construction on the branch, the shelter having no windows. Llandogo retained its own stopping place until closure of the railway.

St Briavels

St Briavels station held the record on the line for name alterations, being renamed no less than three times. The station was built in 1876 and was originally named Bigsweir, after the bridge on the River Wye that the station was neighbour to. It was then decided that the station should be named after a village, as was the case with the other three stations on the line. Therefore in May 1909 the station was renamed St Briavels and Llandogo, St Briavels being the nearest, largest village, situated just over a mile from the railway. The final re-naming came on 1st February, 1927 when Llandogo was dropped from the title in anticipation of the opening of Llandogo Halt.

Llandogo Halt on a crisp winter morning. The photograph is taken from a carriage window of the SLS Special on 4th January, 1959   *J. Hodge*

An afternoon Monmouth-Chepstow freight train near Llandogo on 30th August, 1960.
                                                                            R.O. Tuck

St Briavels station looking north on 2nd January, 1959. The train in the platform is headed by a pannier tank. Note the containers in the wagons in the good yard (*right*). *Derek Chaplin*

St Briavels station. *Reproduced from the 25", 1921 Ordnance Survey Map*

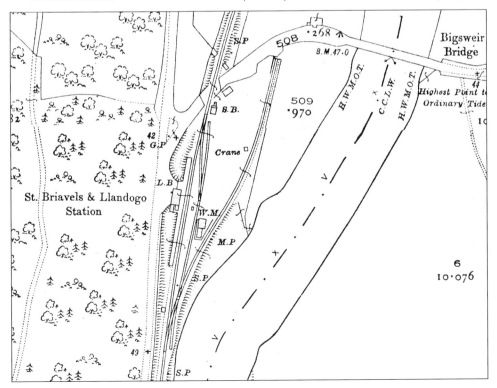

'St Briavels and Llandogo' reads the station sign in this view looking towards Monmouth.

R.S. Carpenter

Whitebrook Halt, view looking towards Tintern on 4th January, 1959.   *Arthur Day*

St Briavels consisted of the station buildings, goods shed, signal box, storage shed and the only level crossing on the route from Monmouth to Chepstow protecting the A466 road. The station was closed to passenger and freight traffic in January 1959. The station and goods shed mostly remain on the site, along with remnants of the distant signal post. The crossing gates were removed completely and replaced with wire fencing.

Whitebrook Halt

Whitebrook Halt was opened on 1st February, 1927 and it was the first of the six halts on the line to be opened by the GWR. Whitebrook had been the location for paper making in the Wye Valley. Three paper mills were situated there, attracted by the softness and purity of the stream water. Paper making ceased in Whitebrook in the 1880s.

Penallt Halt

Without doubt the closest stopping places on the branch were Penallt Halt and Redbrook-on-Wye station. They were only separated by Penallt viaduct. The viaduct was sometimes referred to, quite wrongly, by some local Victorian newspapers as Redbrook railway bridge. Penallt Halt was opened on 1st August, 1931 and remained in use until the closure of the line. The village of Penallt was famous for producing millstones of very high quality due to a type of exceptionally hard 'pudding stone' quarried locally.

Penallt Halt, view looking south in 1966. *Lens of Sutton*

Pannier tank No. 3726 is seen on Penallt viaduct on 3rd January, 1959, the last day of ordinary passenger services. Penallt Halt is in the distance and 'The Boat' public house on the right. The viaduct remains as a support for the adjacent footbridge.   *R.O. Tuck*

Penallt viaduct viewed from Chapel Lane. On the extreme left we can see the handrails at the end of the platform at Penallt Halt. Across the river is Redbrook station, with the goods shed visible.   *Provenance Unknown*

Pannier tank No. 3726 has crossed the River Wye and enters Redbrook station on 3rd January, 1959, with the 1.40 pm Newport-Monmouth service.   *R.O. Tuck*

Redbrook-on-Wye

Redbrook-on-Wye station was built during the construction of the railway; during its 83 years of years of service, the station won numerous prizes for its attractive flower beds and climbing roses. This colourful spectacle became a well known landmark with the valley communities and visitors along the branch. Redbrook's village name was taken from red stones that appear in a stream that runs through the village and into the Wye. The stones are not found elsewhere in the Wye Valley. Redbrook's railway complex consisted of a station building, goods shed and signal box, which controlled the loop and sidings that were situated at the southern end of the platform. By October 1925 the signal box was manned only when required, as the sidings were only occasionally used. The entire site was demolished in the late 1960s and a restaurant which soon occupied the site of the old station has now also disappeared. A GWR boundary post marked the southern border of Redbrook sidings.

Nine years after opening of the railway an old tinplate works that was previously owned by the Redbrook Tinplate Co. was revitalised under the new ownership of David Nurse. The new company pioneered methods of rolling tinplate into extremely thin strips. It was reported in the WVR Minute book of shareholders' meetings that the new tinplate works would provide a much needed source of revenue. Unfortunately the tinplate works did not prosper to any great degree, but nevertheless managed to produce a steady output until 1961, when the works finally shut, bringing to a close a long history of metal working at Lower Redbrook.

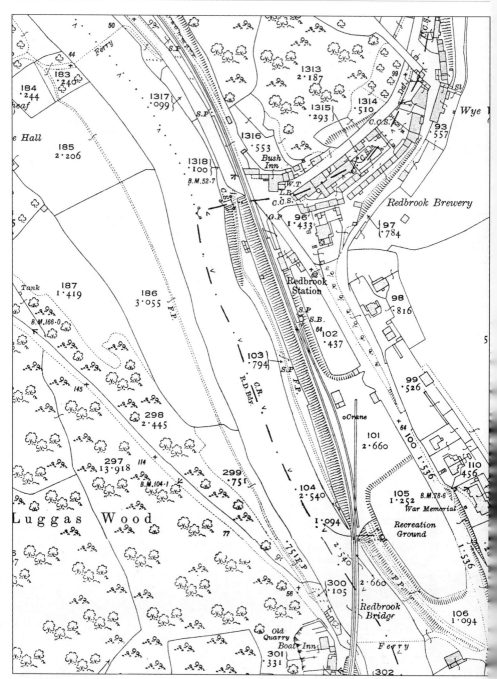

Redbrook station.   *Reproduced from the 25", 1921 Ordnance Survey Map*

A pannier tank is seen at Redbrook about to depart for Chepstow on the early afternoon train
from Monmouth in November 1958. *Derek Chaplin*

An early view of Redbrook station and staff. *Courtesy Mrs Mackenzie*

Pannier tank No. 7774 at Redbrook with a passenger train on 3rd January, 1959.   *R.O. Tuck*

Redbrook after closure.   Vandals have already turned their attention to the windows of the ground frame.   *Lens of Sutton*

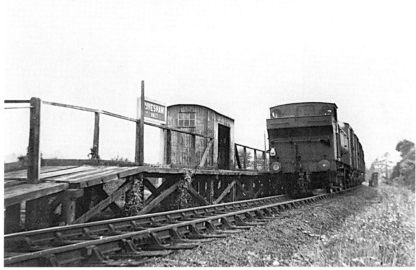

A pannier tank trundles past Wyesham Halt with a Monmouth to Chepstow goods train.
Arthur Day

Wyesham Halt

Wyesham Halt was opened on 12th January, 1931 and remained open to passengers until 5th January, 1959. The halt was situated immediately south of a bridge that carried the railway over the A466 road. Wyesham Halt and bridge have both now been removed and there is virtually no evidence of their existence. From Wyesham to Monmouth the line had been built by the Coleford, Monmouth, Usk & Pontypool Railway in 1861 (*see Appendix Two*).

Monmouth Troy

Troy station was built by the Coleford, Monmouth, Usk & Pontypool Railway and opened for traffic in 1857. As other railways forged their way towards Monmouth (Ross & Monmouth 1874; Wye Valley, 1876; Coleford branch, 1883) the station began to grow in importance and in its heyday it was a busy rural junction. There were other railways planned to reach Troy. The first was the Worcester, Dean Forest & Monmouth Railway of 1863. The first sod of this railway was cut, but unfortunately all the available finance was lost in complex Parliamentary wrangles. The second scheme was called the Monnow Valley project of 1865 which was intended to construct the line from Monmouth to Pontrilas. Tunnel excavations began at Monmouth but were soon halted. The Monnow Valley line fell foul of bankruptcy when its main contractor Thomas Savin went to the wall. The last scheme, and the most grandiose, was the

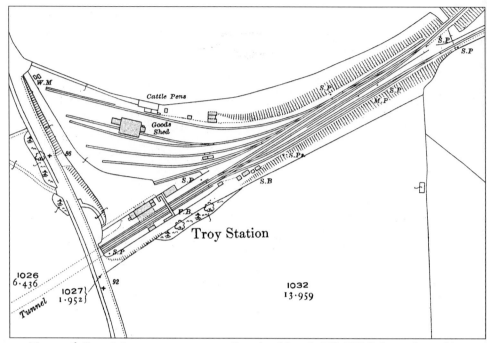

Monmouth Troy station.   *Reproduced from the 25", 1921 Ordnance Survey Map*

A view of Monmouth Troy station in 1922 looking east. The Wye Valley branch approaches the station from the right across Joseph Firbank's viaduct, with the Ross-on-Wye and Hereford line disappearing off to the left.   *R.S. Carpenter*

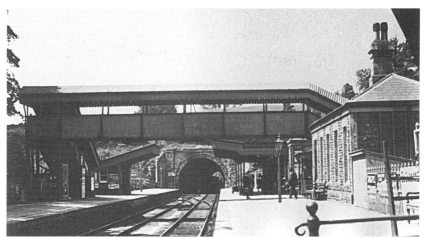

Monmouth Troy station, again in the 1922, looking west towards the tunnel and Pontypridd.   *R.S. Carpenter*

Midland, Monmouth & Severn Bridge Junction Railway of 1885. This was a plan put forward by the Midland Railway to thrust its metals into the heart of Great Western territory; the route was surveyed but the line never materialised.

Troy station with its four pleasant country branches has been unfortunate inasmuch as it only just missed out on becoming a main line junction station, if railway development had taken a different course. If the north/south-west trunk main line from Crewe via Shrewsbury and Hereford had taken the natural route down the Wye Valley through Monmouth (which incidentally is about 15 miles shorter than the route through Abergavenny), or if the South

A quiet scene at Monmouth Troy which provides a good view of the station frontage.
Arthur Day

Main station buildings on the eastbound platform at Monmouth Troy, June 1956.   *Arthur Day*

Platform shelter on the westbound platform at Monmouth Troy.   *Arthur Day*

The view from the signal box of the goods yard at Monmouth Troy in June 1956.

Arthur Day

Wales main line had run from Gloucester through to Monmouth and then continued to Newport, or finally if the Irish traffic had branched off at Monmouth to go through Abergavenny, Brecon and Llandovery, a shorter line than that taken: Troy would have been central to all these possibilities. A new housing estate now occupies most of the old station site. The remainder lies derelict and overgrown. The bricked-up tunnel is the only visible remnant of the Coleford, Monmouth, Usk & Pontypool Railway.

Monmouth Troy goods shed in May 1976.   *B.M. Handley*

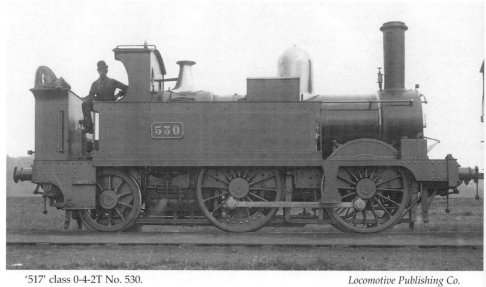

'517' class 0-4-2T No. 530.   *Locomotive Publishing Co.*

'Metro' class 2-4-0T No. 469 at Tintern *circa* 1912.   *Real Photographs*

Chapter Seven

Motive Power

From the opening of the Wye Valley line the GWR was responsible for the motive power and rolling stock and, being a branch line, the locomotives were generally of the '517' class light tank engine introduced by Joseph Armstrong (CME of the GWR 1864-1877). These excellent locomotives built at Wolverhampton from 1868-1885 were the 0-4-2 branch line tank engines recognisable by their burnished brass domes, round-eyed windows and jaunty-shaped, copper-capped chimneys. Some years later in 1895 there were several more modifications to the class, these innovations including outside bearings for the trailing wheels. The boiler pressures varied from 150-165 lb. developing a tractive effort between 12,635 lb. to a maximum of 14,780 lb. Two types of cylinder sizes were used, 16 in. x 24 in. and 16½ in. x 24 in.; the valve gear was of the Stephenson type. The first locomotive was withdrawn from service in 1904, but the class continued to operate until 1945 when the last locomotive was withdrawn.

A total of 149 of GWR 'Metropolitan' class 2-4-0Ts were built over a 30 year period from 1869. The Armstrong and Dean 'Metros' got their name from their main duty, which was working the London Metropolitan lines. Many were fitted with condensing apparatus for long tunnel working. The class was divided into three types according to their Belpaire boiler size as follows: small (boiler type 'S0'), medium (boiler type 'S2') and large (boiler type 'S4'). There were also detailed construction differences. There were four different coal bunkers and five different cabs used throughout the class. All locomotives had 5 ft driving wheels and 16 in. x 24 in. cylinders. Many of the class were fitted with auto-gear for branch line push/pull working. In 1913, 'Metro' class No. 461 could be seen working the Wye Valley line from its shed base at Severn Tunnel Junction. In July 1914, T.B. Peacock describes in his essay 'A Trip by the Wye Valley Train', a journey along the Wye Valley pulled by a 'Metro' class 2-4-0T locomotive. The last member of this class was withdrawn from service in 1949.

These attractive little tanks remained with the Wye Valley branch virtually unchanged until the early 1930s when, under the direction of Charles B. Collett, most of the early Victorian branch line locomotives were replaced by modified and improved designs of which the '48XX' (later '14XX') and '64XX' tank classes were examples. These new locomotives were larger and more powerful and, being fitted with larger coal bunkers than the '517' class, were capable of longer turns of duty before having to refuel. The majority of the new locomotives were fitted with push-pull apparatus which made them ideal for single line working.

The Dean '1076' class 0-6-0T 'Buffalo' class, Nos. 754, 1180, 1254 and 1637, were also seen on the Wye Valley branch. This class of double-framed tank engines with 4 ft 6 in. driving wheels had been built between 1870 and 1884. As built they had 140 lb. boiler pressure, cylinders 17 in. x 24 in. and tractive effort was 15,285 lb. Throughout the history of the Wye Valley line there was only one officially recorded accident, this involved '1076' class No. 1254 which became derailed near Whitebrook Halt on 7th March, 1929.

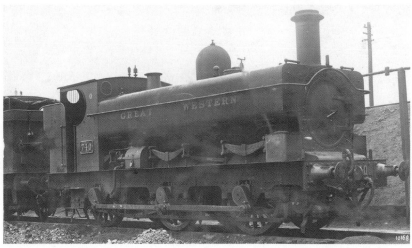

'1076' or 'Buffalo' class 0-6-0T No. 740 seen here with pannier tanks (fitted in 1914).
Locomotive Publishing Co.

Between 1932 and 1936 the new '48XX' class 0-4-2 tanks were turned out at Swindon: they weighed just over 41 tons and had 5 ft 2 in. driving wheels with 16 in. x 24 in. cylinders. The boiler had a working pressure of 165 psi delivering a tractive effort of 13,900 lb. These locomotives having a tractive effort below 16,500 lb. were ungrouped and were more or less unrestricted in their route capabilities. Newport Ebbw Jn, Pontypool Road and Hereford were the sheds that served the Wye Valley branch, and they were assigned several

MAXIMUM SPEED OF TRAINS THROUGH JUNCTIONS AND AT OTHER SPECIFIED PLACES—*continued.*

Name of Place.	From	To	Miles per hour
CHEPSTOW AND MONMOUTH.			
Wye Valley Junction	Main Line	Wye Valley Line and vice versa	10
Tintern Station	ʃ Chepstow	Monmouth	10
	ˋ Monmouth	Chepstow	10
Between Monmouth (Troy) and Redbrook 13m. 46ch. and 13m. 39ch.	Monmouth	Chepstow and vice versa ..	20

Maximum Loads for Main Line Freight Trains

SECTION.		WORKING LOADS. Maximum number of wagons to be conveyed except by Trains specially provided for in the Service Books or by arrangement.	MAXIMUM ENGINE LOADS											
			For Group **A** Engines.				For Group **B** Engines.				For Group **C** Engines.			
From	To		Class 1 Traffic.	Class 2 Traffic.	Class 3 Traffic.	Empties.	Class 1 Traffic.	Class 2 Traffic.	Class 3 Traffic.	Empties.	Class 1 Traffic.	Class 2 Traffic.	Class 3 Traffic.	Empties.
UP.														
Chepstow . ..	Tintern	50	15	18	23	30	17	20	26	34	19	23	29	38
Tintern	Redbrook ..	50	26	31	39	52	30	45	60	64	32	38	48	64
Redbrook.. ..	Monmouth Troy	50	18	22	27	36	21	25	32	42	22	26	33	44
DOWN.														
Monmouth Troy	Redbrook ..	50	15	18	23	30	17	20	34		19	23	29	38
Redbrook ..	Tintern	50	36	43	54	60	42	50	63	80	45	54	68	85
Tintern	Chepstow ..	50	18	22	27	36	21	25	32	42	22	26	33	44

of the new tanks of which Nos. 1421, 1445, 1455 were to stay with the Wye Valley branch until its closure, sharing daily duties with 0-6-0 pannier tanks mainly of the '64XX' class, also built at Swindon during the same period. These were heavier locomotives than the '14XX' class weighing 45 tons 12 cwt., but their driving wheels were slightly smaller at 4 ft 7½ in. They were fitted with 16½ in. x 24 in. cylinders and produced a boiler pressure of 165 lb. psi. This gave the locomotives a working tractive effort of 16,510 lb. qualifying the class for power class 'A' and a yellow route restriction colour. Nos. 6412, 6415, 6426, 6430, 6439 were examples of the class that were assigned duties along the branch. The saddest duty in the history of the branch was given to two pannier tanks of this class, numbers 6412 and 6439. They pulled the last passenger train between Monmouth and Chepstow. The latter of the two locomotives was lucky enough to escape the fate of the breakers' yard when it was withdrawn from service in November 1964. It was purchased for preservation by the Dart Valley Railway where it stayed until 1972, when it was transferred to the Torbay Steam Railway to operate along the former seven mile GWR line between Paignton and Kingswear. In 1976 it went to the West Somerset Railway.

The '14XX' and '64XX' classes were occasionally supplemented by '57XX' class tanks and, a fireman, Mr Fuller of Portskewett, who worked on the branch in the late 1930s told me he could remember cooking breakfast on his shovel in the sidings at various times on two '57XX' class tanks, Nos. 5714 and 9745.

During the 1930s the Wye Valley, like so many other branch lines up and down the country, saw the introduction of the auto-trailer. This was a passenger vehicle that had a special driver's compartment at one end fitted out with a steam regulator, brake and other controls so that if the coach was leading in direction of travel the train could be driven from the separate driving compartment. These new auto-trains provided a basic economy in time and fuel as the locomotive did not have to uncouple and 'run-round' at each terminus. The units themselves were 60 ft long and 9 ft wide and had a carrying capacity of 56 passengers. All major railways made some use of these push-pull auto-trains or auto-cars, the GWR having the most, employing them on many of its picturesque country routes. Nos. W153W, W174W and W237W were regularly scheduled turns of duty along the Wye Valley line towards the end of the 1950s.

STANDARD LOADS OF PASSENGER, PARCELS AND FISH TRAINS FOR ENGINE WORKING PURPOSES.

SECTION		3300-3455 4400 4410 4500-4599 5500-5574 57, 77, 87 & 97XX	3252-3291 1003-1013 2251-2280 0-6-2 T "B" Group—	0-6-0 & 0-6-0 T. 0-6-2 T. A Group.	3210 to 3225 1119-1128	2-4-0 T. Metro 0-4-2T. 48 & 58XX 898 900 908 910	0-4-2 T (517 Class) 1334 1335 1336
FROM	To						
		Tons	Tons	Tons	Tons	Tons	Tons
Monmouth	Ross	310	—	260	260	220	200
Ross	Monmouth	310	—	260	260	220	200
Chepstow	Tintern	225	—	175 200§	—	140	120
Tintern	Monmouth	225	—	175 200§	—	160	140
Monmouth	Pontypool Road	240 249§	—	190 224§	—	170	150

Pannier tank No. 6439 takes water at Monmouth Troy in 1956.   *Arthur Day*

'14XX' class No. 1445 is ready for departure with the 6.05 pm to Ross-on-Wye, note the cattle wagon at the rear. Behind this train stands pannier tank No. 6431 with the 6.20 pm to Newport via the Wye Valley line, 9th May, 1958.   *R.O. Tuck*

Railcar No. 23 was one of a batch built in 1940. It is seen here arriving at Monmouth Troy with the 6.01 pm from Chepstow on 12th September, 1949. The auto-train for Ross-on-Wye can be seen in the opposite platform.   *R.J. Buckley*

Steam did not altogether have the exclusive rights for the Wye Valley line; from the mid-1930s onwards the diesel engine began to make an appearance on many little used routes. This new mode of rail transport took the form of the diesel railcar, and No. 30 was first assigned to the Wye Valley branch during the early part of 1941. Railcar construction began in 1933 and No. 30 was one of a complement of 38 built after that date. The bodies were built by Park Royal Coachworks Ltd. The engines and chassis were built by the Associated Equipment Co. (AEC) at their Southall works. For Nos. 19-38 the engines consisted of two direct injection, 121 hp units of 120 mm bore and 142 mm stroke, giving 210 brake horsepower. The bogie units had a wheel base of 8 ft 6 in. and the centres were 43 ft 6 in. apart. The wheels were of 3 ft 2 in. diameter. The cars were fitted with standard draw gear and mechanical transmission; 15 of the cars (intended for branch lines) were geared down to give a maximum speed of 40 mph in order to provide sufficient tractive effort for hauling a tail load of up to 60 tons. The seating arrangements varied between the cars, from a low figure of 44 to a maximum of 70.

Much later in the working life of the railway diesel power was to make frequent visits, albeit at the southern end on duties to Tidenham Quarry. The most powerful of the visitors were class '37' built between 1960 and 1965. Their 12-cylinder power units were English Electric and of 1,750 bhp. The locomotives weighed 106 tons and produced a tractive effort of 55,500 lb. Other visitors were English Electric type '2', class '31', built from 1959 to 1962 which could develop a tractive effort of 42,800 lb. and the diesel-hydraulic Beyer, Peacock class '35' 'Hymeks' introduced in 1961, powered by engines built by Bristol-Siddeley-Maybach and weighing 75 tons. The 'Hymeks' were capable of developing a tractive effort of 49,700 lb.

The most popular diesel locomotives on the branch to call at Tidenham Quarry were the 0-6-0 class '14s'. These locomotives were the last British Rail diesel-hydraulic design and were intended for short trip workings. They were ideally suited for country lines such as the Wye Valley line and the remains of the Coleford branch. They were powered by Paxman 6-cylinder engines and produced 650 bhp at 1,500 rpm. They had a maximum tractive effort of 39,910 lb.

Doris Ball is seen as a babe in her mother's arms in this group photograph taken at Llandogo Halt in 1929.   *Doris Ball Collection*

Llandogo halt, view looking towards Tintern.   *Provenance Unknown*

Chapter Eight

Reminiscences

Doris Ball

In the photograph opposite Doris Ball is seen on the platform at Llandogo Halt as a baby in her mother's arms. The four inch sepia picture was taken in 1929 and ever since she has had a love affair with the Wye Valley Railway. When the railway was working Doris and her friends liked to travel up and down the line from Chepstow to Monmouth, taking a ride in the train 'just because' it was such a beautiful run.

As a very young child, Doris remembers always getting very excited when she heard the train coming. The beat of the engine echoed down the valley and the occasional warning blast from the locomotive's whistle signalled its approach. Then the puffs of smoke would appear, and suddenly the locomotive came into view following the meanderings of the river. She and her friends called the engines 'Coffee Pots'. This tradition came about because of a vertical boilered locomotive that was used along the Wireworks branch of the railway at Tintern. Later, in the 1940s, Doris and her friends used to catch the train regularly to attend school in Monmouth. The timetable was very convenient to get to the lessons on time. Even now, 50 years later, Doris can still remember the times when the trains arrived at Llandogo Halt.

8.25 am to Monmouth Troy	9.25 am to Chepstow
11.25 am to Monmouth Troy	12.25 pm to Chepstow
3.25 pm to Monmouth Troy	4.25 pm to Chepstow
5.25 pm to Monmouth Troy	6.25 pm to Chepstow

There were no service trains on Sundays, but in the summer special excursion trains called going to all sorts of places. Doris and her family used to catch these if they were heading to the seaside for a day's outing.

On Saturdays Doris sometimes went with her mother shopping in Monmouth, going on the train as a change from the bus. However, this meant a very long walk from Monmouth Troy station, situated on the far outskirts of town, to the shops. It was all right if you didn't have heavy loads to carry. During the terrible winter of 1947 no buses ran for weeks, but the good old trains of the Wye Valley Railway kept on steaming through and never let the local community down.

Llandogo Halt was always fairly busy but particularly in the summer months when the 3.25 pm would arrive from Chepstow on a Saturday afternoon. This increased traffic was because there used to be a very popular holiday fellowship guest house in the village, this was situated up a steep hill from the halt. The farmer's son used to meet this train with a horse and cart to pick up a huge pile of suitcases and other luggage the passengers brought with them.

In regard to goods, parcels etc. these would normally never be off-loaded at Llandogo, which was 'only' a halt. The goods van was on the rear of the train and

The Temperance Hall at Woodcroft. *Woodcroft Christian Centre*

The slate-topped bar still exists in the coffee tavern. *R. Dingwall*

so if you wanted something dispatched or collected it meant going to Chepstow, Tintern, Bigsweir (later 'St Briavels'), Redbrook or Monmouth Troy. Tidenham, Brockweir, Llandogo, Whitebrook and Wyesham were 'halts' and didn't have the necessary facilities.

As a little girl, Doris remembers her uncle sending her a sweet little puppy in a basket all the way from Bristol. She had to walk a mile to Bigsweir station to collect the tiny creature. The station master at Bigsweir station was Charles Fox. Doris has very fond memories of Charles. He was a lovely and most helpful man, who fed and watered the puppy until she arrived to pick him up. Charles Fox is well remembered in Llandogo where he lived in a house provided by the railway. Before Mr Fox a Mr Saunders ran the station.

Phyllis Hughes

Mrs Phyllis Hughes also has many fond memories of the Wye Valley Railway; she was born at Abbey Farm in Tintern in 1915. The first facts that Phyllis discovered about the railway go back to the date of its building in 1874 and 1875 when some of the engineers responsible for the line stayed with her grandparents at Coed Ithal Farm during the week, going home at the weekends. The line ran at the bottom of their fields.

On the other hand the navvies, mostly from Ireland, were a hard-drinking crowd and on pay day they headed for the cider houses of Chepstow, spending much of their wages in just a few hours. Chepstow had a good number of taverns and easily catered for the increased demand. The drunken scenes disgusted Christiana Morgan and so when her husband, Thomas Henry Morgan, died in 1877 she had a memorial Temperance Hall built to honour his name. This was erected in the nearby village of Woodcroft. In the Hall was a coffee tavern, a reading room, and a lending library offering Christian literature. Today the Temperance Hall is known as the Woodcroft Christian Centre, it still has the original coffee room and its slate-topped bar. A strict condition on present visitors to the Hall is that no alcohol must be consumed.

From September 1927 to July 1933 Phyllis attended Monmouth High School (now known as Haberdashers Monmouth School for Girls) and travelled daily on the Wye Valley trains. Until September 1929, when Brockweir Halt was opened, Phyllis used to walk from her home down to Brockweir Valley and along the road to Tintern station, quite a considerable distance. The schoolchildren got to know the guards on the trains quite well, the officials would occasionally inspect season tickets and if pupils were late would hold up the train for a couple of minutes, until they arrived exhausted from having run the last 100 yards or so.

The boys, attending a separate nearby school in Monmouth (also a Haberdashers School), alighted at Wyesham Halt after it opened in 1931; they were often segregated from the girls on the train. The school train Phyllis caught left Chepstow around 7.55 am and arrived at Tintern at 8.15 am. It then stopped at Bigsweir and Redbrook stations and lastly Monmouth Troy. A long walk followed, in crocodile fashion, across Chippenham through St Mary's Churchyard and up the Hereford Road to school.

William Davies, Monmouth Troy station master, 1927.   *Gladys Allen Collection*

On Fridays there were considerably more passengers carried due to a produce market in Monmouth, quite a few housewives using the train to do their weekly shopping. For the most part the womenfolk journeyed home with their fruit and vegetables on the 12 noon service whilst the girls and boys caught the 4.05 pm train.

Sometimes the train would stop in the middle of fields to pick up passengers who had waved the engine down. This was usually on market days. The guard would swiftly haul them aboard. In gratitude the ladies, who otherwise would have missed the train, gave the driver and guard fruit on the return journey and vegetables they had bought from the produce stalls at Monmouth as a reward.

One problem with the Wye Valley Railway was that all the stations were quite a distance from the towns and villages they served; to remedy this problem various halts were built in the late 1920s. These stopping places improved the situation and consisted of very basic galvanised sheds with a wooden seat for five to six people to sit and shelter in, if the weather turned wet. The halts were very welcome and much appreciated, the guards would issue tickets to the people boarding the train at these stops.

Diesel railcars were introduced along the Wye Valley Railway in the early 1940s. The trains were stationed at Severn Tunnel Junction and connected with trains to and from Bristol. This train was known along the Wye Valley as the 'Elver Express', it looked just like a baby eel.

Phyllis remembers the station master at Tintern being Mr A. Davies, with a Mr Mayo in charge of the signal box. Charles Lewis who was once the signalman at Bigsweir station was later promoted to station master at Tintern and was in charge there all through the 1930s.

Gladys Allen

Mrs Gladys Allen relates that her grandfather, William Davies, was the station master at Monmouth Troy station, serving from 1919 until 1928 when he retired from the railways. Mr Davies ran the station like clockwork, he was always very strict in having things done correctly. If a train was late for any reason the driver had to explain why. This discipline made the Wye Valley Railway into an excellent service and nobody had any cause for complaint. People living beside the line used to time their comings and goings by the trains as they were so reliable.

Another matter William Davies took pride in was the appearance of the station, it was always beautifully kept with lovely gardens and flowers all the season round. May Hill station (at Monmouth) was also under Mr Davies' control and Mrs Allen remembers being given a footplate ride on the steam engine between the two stations when she was five years old. Mr Davies won his first station master's hat at the age of 21, the youngest-ever station master on the GWR in those days. By the time he retired he had worn out 21 hats - quite an achievement! Mrs Allen's mother and aunt were also employed at Monmouth Troy station working in the booking office. A proper railway family.

Our Chepstow-bound shopping special emerges from Tidenham tunnel to stop at Netherhope
Halt.   *Iris Knight Family Collection*

An old picture postcard view of Chepstow station. The station was designed by W. Lancaster
Owen and the footbridge built by Edward Finch & Co. in 1892.   *Provenance Unknown*

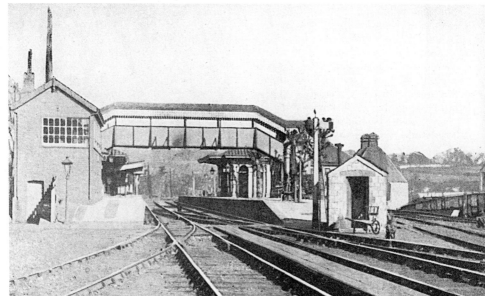

Iris Knight

Mrs Knight was born in 1917 at Boughspring in the country north of Netherhope. Her father was a nursery man and market gardener. As a young girl she recalls various adventures with her friends along the route of the Wye Valley Railway, the earliest being the long walks from her home to see the trains. The path would take her over fields and a stone stile, through a small wood, in which wild garlic grew, this produced an unforgettable aroma.

The track came out onto Netherhope Lane near an overbridge which looked down onto the southern portal of Tidenham tunnel. If a train could be heard rumbling through the tunnel she would always try and get somebody to hoist her up to peer over the parapet to see the train emerging with all its billowing smoke. It was always an exciting event, especially when the driver whistled and waved. On the other side of the bridge and over another stile a narrow path threaded its way to Tidenham, a long, never-ending walk for a small child.

In those days Tidenham was a station with its own station master, 'little' Mr Edwards as the children of the day called him. Mrs Knight recalls catching a train from here for the annual outing to Weston-super-Mare via the Severn Tunnel. In 1932 Netherhope Halt was built outside Tidenham tunnel. This saved an awful lot of shoe leather and needless to say the train was always boarded from here after its opening.

The train was always in constant use for shopping expeditions in Chepstow, that was until the 'Bristol Blue' bus started running services. The bus stop was much closer and so much more convenient. However, after galloping up to the Coleford Road Mrs Knight would often see the back of the bus disappearing. Missed it yet again! At least the four daily trains could be relied upon even though they were not regular enough, and it meant a much longer trek.

A ventilation shaft just about halfway along the mile-long tunnel protruded a short distance from the Coleford Road, the funnel is still there today. It used to be surrounded by Walkhope Woods which unfortunately no longer exist. Amongst the trees was a secret source of 'butterfly orchids' which were very rare indeed. Mrs Knight remembers they had a wonderful scent. Bee orchids grew there too and masses of bluebells. She says: 'Us kids used to play around the stony wall of the air vent which was much too high for us to climb, and by chance often heard the steam engine rumbling far beneath our feet; this was followed by a whiff of smoke from the top of the shaft'.

By coincidence, many years on in life, after marrying a rail ganger who worked on the Chepstow length of main line for 40 years, Iris got a surprise. Her husband came home one day as usual for tea and announced that, as he lived locally, he had been instructed to walk through and check the condition of Netherhope tunnel. Being claustrophobic he dreaded it, so Mrs Knight volunteered to accompany him. They went together across the fields to Netherhope Halt. Switching on their torches they entered the tunnel, hand in hand. A wind blew at the entrance but petered out after a short distance. The tunnel was bricked for a considerable way but, she remembers, there were plenty of recesses in the walls for gangers to shelter in to avoid any speeding trains. About halfway, near the eerie shadows of the air vent, the walls of the

View looking into Tidenham tunnel.
R. Dingwall

The top of the air shaft at Tidenham tunnel.
R. Dingwall

Ex-GWR Collett '14XX' class 0-4-2T No. 1421 at Severn Tunnel Junction. This locomotive was a regular performer on the Wye Valley passenger trains which originated from here.
Provenance Unknown

tunnel became natural rock; it was a strange feeling but at long last she managed to look up the ventilation shaft she played around as a child on the surface all those years ago. Continuing, they followed the curve of the track until the darkness changed to a dull grey and suddenly a blinding white speck of light. They had made it to the far end where a hazardous zig-zag path took them out just below the Cockshoot and safely home again.

Cyril Goulding

Cyril started in 1937 as a cleaner and later became a fireman and then driver before he finished his service on the Wye Valley Railway in 1952. Before he retired a typical day's duty for Cyril started when he arrived at 6 am at Ebbw Junction. The engine shed was situated on the north side of the main line about a mile west of Newport station. The shed code on the engines located here was 86A. Reporting in at the duty clerk's office Cyril picked up his check No. 476, a small oval bronze disc, which had to be handed back in at the end of the day's work.

A glance at the roster sheet pinned on the wall told Cyril what engine was booked out for him that day. As often as not it was a '14XX' class locomotive, this had a short wheelbase enabling it to manoeuvre around the tight curves on the Wye Valley line. The '14XX' class were ideal and extremely suitable for the task ahead in every way.

Having found the engine in the gloom of the shed he would be pleased to see that it would have been partially prepared for him to drive, the locomotive simmering away just ready for oiling up. With care, a full water tank was just enough to get the train to Monmouth, here the tank would be replenished for the return journey. The engine burnt six tons of coal over the 10½ hour period before Cyril returned to the locomotive shed after a hard day's work.

There would be no time to admire the views, 148 miles had to be covered. The train crew had to eat their sandwiches as they went along. Leaving the shed at 6.45 am, clearance was given to go down the line to High Street, Newport station and pick up the coaches. After the fireman coupled-up, Cyril waited at the platform ready to leave at exactly 7.05 am to Severn Tunnel Junction and the start of the Wye Valley timetabled services, stopping at all halts and stations to Monmouth Troy.

It was normal practice that two coaches would be pulled behind the engine to Monmouth, and then propelled in front of the locomotive back down to Chepstow. On very busy days, at Easter for example, the train would be made up with two coaches in the front of the engine and two behind. The driver then sat in a special compartment in the leading carriage, this was fitted with a regulator and a brake. This method of operating is called auto-working and avoids the engine having to run round its train at each terminus. Only the driver would change position. The fireman, who in case of emergency could also drive the train, meanwhile kept the fire going and maintained boiler pressure on the engine. A bell code system linked him to the driver at the front of the train.

At one time there were two Chepstow stations: Chepstow West or Main station built in 1850 and Chepstow East at Snipe Hill, Tidenham. What separated them was a two hour journey by coach and horses and the thick

Chepstow station and staff in broad gauge days.   *Chepstow Museum*

The raising of Chepstow station in 1877 to accommodate the trains for the Wye Valley Railway.
Chepstow Museum

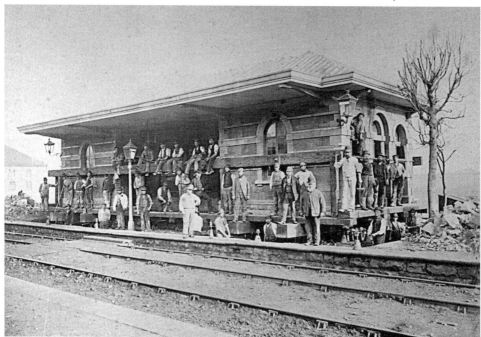

muddy waters of the River Wye Estuary. Brunel's tubular suspension bridge eventually linked the two sections together and so connected South Wales to London by rail for the first time. The single-line bridge was opened on Monday 19th July, 1852. The 600 ft long bridge was the prototype for Brunel's famous bridge over the River Tamar at Saltash, and drew many visitors to admire its tall and unusual design.

The crossing of the river posed many problems with limestone cliffs on the Gloucester side of the river and a bed of oozing mud on the other. There was also the problem of very rapid high tides to overcome, a 50 ft clearance being required above the highest water level. Brunel found the solution by building the tubular suspension bridge. It was a masterpiece of boldness and ingenuity.

The main 309 ft railway-span was suspended from diagonal chains hung from the tubes, these in turn were laid on twin towers erected on the firm rocky foundations on the Gloucestershire bank. The other end of the wrought-iron tubes, which were 9 ft in diameter, rested on six cylinders sunk into the river bed. The contractor was Messrs Finch & Willet from Liverpool. They had a site just beside the bridge for all the ironwork involved in its building.

After the bridge was completed the men employed stayed in the yard and started building ships, thus transforming the whole area around the bridge. The shipyards became an ever-changing vista for Cyril as he steamed past, by then they had already gone through various stages of development, first becoming National Shipyard No. 1, forming a part of the Government national action scheme, and when this failed to work, the Monmouth Ship Building Co. took them over.

After 110 years, Brunel's tubular suspension bridge was dismantled in 1962 and replaced by new spans. This work was carried out for British Railways by Fairfield Shipbuilding & Engineering Co., the latest occupiers of the shipyards.

With the opening of the Wye Valley Railway in 1876 Chepstow station became a busy junction. It was not made any easier by the fact that the platform levels at Chepstow were nearly 3 feet lower than the carriages. This difficulty caused many complaints from irate passengers at the time. Tiring of the situation, in 1877, the GWR finally arranged to increase the height of the platforms, however two station buildings stood in their way. The remedy was to jack up the buildings brace on massive timbers to the new height, and then raise the platforms underneath.

Upon crossing the brown-stained waters of the River Wye the main line continued into a wide cutting to enter Wye Valley Junction (Tutshill Halt). Just prior to this halt, long ago the terminus of Chepstow East had been situated. The beginning of the Wye Valley branch started with a steeply rising spur climbing up at 1 in 66 to the left of the main line.

Going on, Cyril was always pleased to get to the top of the gradient where a bridge over the line meant he could gently ease back on the regulator. After a short straight section the next stage of the journey took the train round a bend to head north along a 10 ft high embankment between fields of waving yellow corn, or perhaps cows with heads bowed eating lush grass. As usual it was customary for a mini-stampede to take place on the approach of the train; at a safe distance the cows would stop and look back at the strange beast within their midst.

The first of a sequence of four photographs of Chepstow station taken *circa* 1964. This view looks towards Severn Tunnel Junction. An ex-GWR pannier tank is visible in the distance.

Nelson Collection

A view along the deserted platforms at Chepstow looking towards Severn Tunnel Junction. Note the stone wagons behind the station nameboard. The nameboard itself now reads just 'CHEPSTOW' all references to the Wye Valley line having been removed (*see photograph page 139*).

Nelson Collection

The photographer stands next to the signal box in this view along the platforms looking towards Gloucester. *Nelson Collection*

A view from the eastern end of Chepstow station looking towards Gloucester showing the sweeping curve onto the bridge (*just visible in the distance*) over the River Wye. By this date Brunel's tubular suspension bridge had been replaced by new spans. *Nelson Collection*

A picture postcard view of Brunel's tubular suspension bridge at Chepstow.

Provenance Unknown

Another view of the tubular suspension bridge.

Chepstow Museum

After ¾ mile the green-painted crushing plant of Dayhouse Quarry hove into view, a simple narrow bridge over the A48 led the line towards the workings and Tidenham station. A run-round loop controlled by ground frames meant wagons could be shunted here to gain access to a goods shed and a short siding.

Departing Tidenham station the track went directly north for ¾ of a mile in a continuous deep cutting. Looking out of the windows of the carriages some unusual plants would be spotted growing in the limestone escarpments. Cyril recalls the tempting blackberries along this section of track before he pulled into Netherhope Halt.

Ahead lay the gaping mouth of Tidenham tunnel a dark cavern some 1,188 yards-long. Carriage windows would hastily be raised to avoid compartments being filled with sulphurous smoke. Cyril was occasionally concerned here, as the locomotives only just fitted into the mouth of the tunnel, and there wasn't any room to stick his head out of the cab. The one thing he remembers to this day about going through the depths of Tidenham tunnel was the tremendous roaring noise the train would make, many others remarked on this too. It was unlike anything else he knew. He wasn't in any doubt it was caused by the solid rock foundations on which the sleepers lay, above the engine there was 150 ft of limestone. Emerging into daylight the train found itself high up on a ledge looking down the steep sides of a cliff into the River Wye far below; this was always a quite dramatic change of scenery which took his breath away.

Cyril didn't have time to admire the view or the many-coloured leaves in the nearby canopy of beech trees for long, because 200 yards ahead were the mineral sidings of Tintern Quarry complete with overhead loading hoppers. A soaring embankment came next connecting a side valley together across its widest point. It was a good job Cyril had a good head for heights, although perhaps he had a few sleepless nights imagining what would happen if he derailed the train here. Probably unknown to Cyril, far below lay a lovely stone drainage adit enabling the valley's stream to drain through the walls of the embankment and flow into the River Wye.

The next obstacle on the journey was Black Morgan viaduct, a three-arch structure again built to link two sides of a depression which the train had to cross. It is the only brick-built viaduct on the line and takes its unusual name from the area of the Forest of Dean in which it is constructed, namely Black Morgan Wood. The name 'Black Morgan' may well be connected with Henry Morgan, who was born in the village of Pencader in Monmouthshire in 1635. As a boy on a visit to Bristol he was kidnapped or 'Barbadosed'. Morgan was taken to America where he was sold as an indentured labourer; after a few years in the employment of wealthy landowners, he escaped and made his way to Jamaica, where he joined seagoing adventurers; by his early 20s he had been involved in many skirmishes with the Spanish. In 1668, aged 28, Morgan took command of his first ship, and became a privateer, this meant he was employed by the English Government to fight the Spaniards on behalf of the King. His pay consisted of booty taken from the Spanish. Henry Morgan was not therefore an outlawed pirate, but a sea raider authorized by an English letter of marque. In 1666 Morgan was elevated to the rank of Admiral, a rapid rate of progress by any measure. In 1668 he organised and successfully carried out assaults and

Wye Valley Junction.

Reproduced from the 25", 1921 Ordnance Survey Map

Wye Valley Junction in 1966. The disused platforms of Tutshill Halt can be seen in the foreground. *Lens of Sutton*

Wye Valley Junction signal box on the right, with an empty stone train ascending the incline to Tintern Quarry on 18th May, 1964. *R.K. Blencowe*

A goods train bound for Chepstow returns the train staff to the signalman at Wye Valley Junction in 1958.   *R.O. Tuck*

Class '37' No. 37238 awaits clearance at the Wye Valley Junction in July 1979 adjacent to the ground frame lever which now controls the points giving access to Tintern Quarry. The up/down main line crossover and points were totally removed following complete closure of the branch in 1992.   *B.M. Handley*

The bridge near the top of the incline where drivers would ease off the regulator to round the sharp left-hand curve in the distance, seen here in 1978. *B.M. Handley*

Shortly after Wye Valley Junction Snipehill bridge carries the railway over a minor road, photographed in 1978. *B.M. Handley*

Pannier tank No. 4657 returns from Tintern Quarry. It is seen on the embankment between the main A48 road and the main line on 18th May, 1964.   *R.K. Blencowe*

An unidentified class '35' 'Hymek' is seen on the overbridge which crosses the A48 *c.* 1969. In 1978 the bridge underwent a major overhaul when the centre sections were strengthened and the sides were reclad in corrugated metal sheet. Tidenham station was situated to the right of the bridge.   *F.A. Blencowe*

Dayhouse Quarry loading operations looking south in 1996.   *R. Dingwall*

Dayhouse Quarry wagon-loading conveyor belt plant at Tidenham, looking north. *R. Dingwall*

A severely overgrown Netherhope Halt, and beyond it, Tidenham tunnel, as it was named by contractors.   *F.A. Blencowe*

Class '14' diesel-hydraulic No. D9508 emerges from Tidenham tunnel with a stone train from Tintern Quarry on 13th April, 1967.   *R.K. Blencowe*

Pannier tank No. 9619 shunts at Tintern Quarry. Guard Arthur Chandler is about to climb aboard the engine, September 1959. *Arthur Day*

Wagons at Tintern Quarry in July 1979. The quarry was owned by W.G. Turrif Ltd. The siding connection was brought into use in February 1931 and consisted of one ground frame to the north of the quarry and a stretch of track leading to the hopper loading bay. This siding remained *in situ* until April 1964 when an additional ground frame was installed, giving a southern access to the sidings. From August 1964 the Wye Valley Junction to Tintern Quarry line was worked as a private siding. The quarry was closed in 1981. *B.M. Handley*

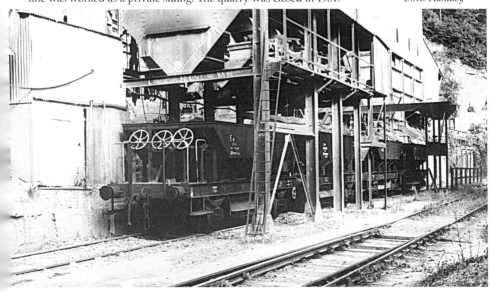

A beautiful brick-lined stream drainage adit below the embankment near Tintern Quarry.
R. Dingwall

Black Morgan viaduct in 1986. The overall length of this structure was 140 ft and it had a width of 19 ft 8 in. The height was 32 ft 2 in., the height of the main arch being 27 ft 2 in. with a span of 26 ft 3 in.   *B.M. Handley*

capture of El Puerto del Principe, and the well garrisoned town of Porto Bello; a year later he raided and captured the harbour town Maracaibo.

In the early 1670s, England was again at odds with Spain and Holland over the rich pickings of the West Indies. King Charles II was informed of the capable and fearless Admiral Morgan and his exploits. The King asked Morgan for advice about the defence of the island of Jamaica. The sugar trade was immensely lucrative and brought in enormous revenue for the Crown, this had to be protected at all costs.

Communications between Henry and the King made great impressions on His Majesty, and for Morgan's successful defence of the Islands the King knighted Morgan in December 1675. At the age of 45 'The King of Buccaneers' Admiral Sir Henry Morgan was acting Governor of Jamaica, Vice Admiral Commandant of the Port Royal Regiment, Judge of the Admiralty Court and Justice of the Peace. With his numerous titles and respectability, Morgan no longer took to the high seas, he settled down to a life of politics and island government, as well as managing his sugar plantations.

Sir Henry Morgan died on 25th August, 1688 and was buried at the Palisadoes, Port Royal, Jamaica. His memory not only survives in the Wye Valley but also on a famous brand of Rum.

Looking north through Tintern tunnel, July 1963.   *Arthur Day*

For approximately the next two miles the railway travelled on a shelf cut in the hillside of Shorn Cliff, the sinuous route still following the course of the River Wye in the valley below. Cyril noted the stone walls built along this part of the railway to hold back the mountains of earth and stop them creeping onto the trackbed.   At one point many stone terraces were constructed above each other to stop a possible landslide, these being more visible in winter months.

Luxuriant vegetation grew thick and fast in this area and had to be continually cut back, this cropping gave rise to one of the Wye Valley Railway's famous legends. What used to happen was that the gangers responsible for looking after the track, cut down the branches and new saplings into particular lengths. These made excellent bean poles. The 'bean sticks' were one of the perks for the gang especially when the embankments were cleared in the spring.

The hazel growth from recent years was chopped down, bundled up and taken to Severn Tunnel Junction in the guard's van. Occasionally full wagon loads found their way unofficially off the railway to be sold elsewhere. Guard's vans would constantly be seen with bean sticks sprouting out through the roof or poking out through windows and doors. Once in a while passengers waiting for their connections would see steam engines arrive with bean poles securely tied to their cladding and bunkers as if they were camouflaged. Everybody seemed to know what was going on. 'It's the Bean Stick Special', they would say. No doubt 'earnings' were divided up later. Officials must have turned a blind eye probably because the clearance of the embankments was an essential safety measure. In the summer months sparks from the locomotives would frequently cause fires and destroy considerable tracts of woodland.

The old branch line at Wireworks Jn was next encountered, although the track itself was lifted in 1941. A walk along the old route replaced the rails. The path started at the Old Corn Mill in Tintern and crossed the River Wye by a bridge close by.

Continuing on, once more the Wye Valley branch entered a second tunnel, this time completely brick-lined, it plunged passengers into darkness for only a short distance. A gentle curve halfway along swung the trackbed to line up with Tintern bridge, which took the railway to the west bank of the Wye. A speed restriction of 5 mph was imposed here.

Fifteen minutes after leaving Chepstow, Cyril steamed into Tintern station to exchange staffs with the signalman. The new staff would give him clearance to carry on to Monmouth in safety knowing that another train would not be on that section of track. Very occasionally extra water would be taken at Tintern. Goods would be swiftly off-loaded for sorting or storing before the train drew out of the station just two minutes after arrival.

The permanent way now continued on the west bank of the River Wye clinging close to its edge, here the alluvium had built up just enough to stop the trackbed from flooding, a serious hazard which needed to be remedied on several occasions.

Brockweir Halt came next, followed by Llandogo Halt, with its cluster of whitewashed cottages arranged against the dark green hillside, and then on to St Briavels station. A ground frame and goods shed were located here.

A Monmouth-bound goods train passing the site of the landslip outside Tintern tunnel. Note strengthening rails outside the running line in the foreground. *Arthur Day*

The former trackbed below Shorn Cliff. *R. Dingwall*

A '14XX' class 0-4-2T heads an auto-train over Tintern bridge. *Granville Williams*

Tintern station looking towards Monmouth on 21st June, 1951, showing GWR diesel railcar No. W30W on the 2.40 pm Chepstow-Monmouth service. *W.A. Camwell*

Pannier tank No. 6426 leaves Brockweir Halt with a train for Severn Tunnel Junction in 1958.
R.O. Tuck

St Briavels station and the River Wye at Bigsweir bridge in June 1962.   *Arthur Day*

A Monmouth-Chepstow goods train pauses at Penallt Halt, whilst guard Arthur Chandler and porter Ted Morgan unload a barrel of beer bound for 'The Boat', the adjacent pub, September 1959. *Arthur Day*

Penallt viaduct in 1996 still standing as a support for a public footbridge and access to 'The Boat' public house. *R. Dingwall*

'14XX' class 0-4-2T No. 1421 stands at Redbrook-on-Wye station with a southbound passenger train.   *Arthur Day*

Men loading tinplate into open wagons at Redbrook.   *Monmouth Museum*

After crossing the A466 on the only level crossing on the railway, located beside Bigsweir's bridge with its toll booth which is still extant, the line became very much easier for the driver. Tiny embankments here and there kept the line level as it went along the flat valley floor. Superb views of the river and hillsides covered in trees made this part of the journey towards Whitebrook Halt quite delightful. Here many paper making mills could be found.

Cuckoo Wood gave way to Hael Wood as the train approached Penallt Halt and its wooden platform. A curving iron girder bridge held up by cast-iron columns took the railway back to the east bank of the river again and into Redbrook station. Redbrook was the location of a tinplate industry. Raw materials were brought into the goods yard to be off-loaded by a crane and then loaded again once processed. Redbrook was a very busy place in its day. Cyril would have had to stop, start and stop again within 200 yards if passengers wanted to leave or join the train at Penallt, this being the distance separating the Halt from Redbrook.

Redbrook station was very attractive. It always had lovely beds of pretty coloured flowers growing continuously all the year round. The station master kept everything neat and tidy. He was always in competition with Tintern station as to which was the best-kept station on the line.

Pulling away from Redbrook station the train proceeded up a gradient to cross the A466 road by a bridge. On the far side the line curved to follow the road on a ledge 100 ft higher, this was well built, huge boulders still lie under the trackbed to give it support and drainage. The water dropped down to the River Wye below where many salmon fishing jetties stick out into its waters.

An old rail and wire fence marked the boundary of the railway as it wound its way through woods towards Wyesham, a signal post can still be found along the route buried in the undergrowth. Before Wyesham Halt a track used to join the Wye Valley Railway from Coleford (see Chapter Ten).

Sometimes the trains rested at Wyesham before the final leg of the journey, once more climbing to cross the A466 again and go over the River Wye by a high bridge with tall stone supports on either side. A 22-arch viaduct on the far side of the river took the railway down into Monmouth Troy station. These imposing structures were designed by Engineer Joseph Firbank (1819-1886) while employed on the construction of the Coleford, Monmouth, Usk and Pontypool Railway. The viaduct was opened on 1st July, 1861, spanning the River Wye near its confluence with the Monnow it carried the railway into Monmouth Troy station for the last ⅕ mile at a steady descent of 1 in 66.

The viaduct, still standing, is a brick and stone structure with 22 semi-elliptical arches, each having a span of almost 30 ft. They in turn were supported on stone piers 5 ft 7 in. wide and 24 ft 6 in. deep. The overall height of the viaduct varied from 26 ft, near the station, rising to almost 50 ft where the track was carried by a single iron span (now removed) across the river. Before reaching the station the line from Monmouth May Hill, Symonds Yat and Ross-on-Wye came in from the right.

Pulling into Troy station the familiar 'All change' was shouted by the guard, there would follow the sound of doors slamming and the porter's luggage trolley being loaded, a few milk churns would be off-loaded and trundled down the platform.

A view of Monmouth from Penallt. The viaduct in the foreground served the Wye Valley Railway and the Coleford branch. The second viaduct is on the Ross and Monmouth Railway.
R. Dingwall Collection

The masonry of the viaduct in 1978, after removal of its central ironwork section. *B.M. Handley*

An auto-train from Chepstow approaches Monmouth. Firbank's viaduct on the right can be seen, while the viaduct on the line to Ross-on-Wye is just visible on the left. *Arthur Day*

Pannier tank No. 6431 takes water at Monmouth Troy prior to departing with the 6.20 pm for Chepstow on 9th September, 1958. *R.O. Tuck*

The eastern end of Monmouth Troy station in 1956 with the signal box to the right. The Wye Valley Railway swings away to the right while the line to the left is for Ross-on-Wye.

Arthur Day

A view looking down on Monmouth Troy station looking east with an auto-train in the platform. The junction for the Wye Valley is alongside the water tank.   *E. Wilmhurst*

Monmouth Troy signal box in June 1956. *Arthur Day*

Signalman Arthur Jarvis stands between two train staff machines in this interior view of Monmouth Troy signal box in 1956. *Arthur Day*

The engine crew hand over the train staff at Monmouth Troy.   *E. Wilmshurst*

'14XX' class 0-4-2T No. 1421 is seen at the tunnel entrance at the western end of Monmouth Troy station.   *Lens of Sutton*

Guard Arthur Chandler is seen on the balcony of an ex-GWR 'Toad' brakevan as a pannier tank performs shunting duties at Monmouth Troy in September 1959. *Arthur Day*

Pannier tank No. 9619 and its train crew in April 1962, driver George Mayo is on the right. *Arthur Day*

WYE VALLEY BRANCH.

Motor Trolley System of Maintenance.

1. This system of maintenance operates from 0 miles 2 chains Wye Valley Junction, to 13 miles 66 chains Monmouth (Troy) and the Standard Instructions relating to the Motor Trolley System of Maintenance shewn on pages 65–68 of the General Appendix to the Rule Book, together with the following special instructions, will apply.

2. The undermentioned engineering gangs will be responsible for that Section of the line :—

No.	Home Station.	m.	ch.	m.	ch.
111	St. Briavels	0	2	11	46
71	Monmouth (Troy)	11	46	13	66

3. Occupation key instruments and telephones are installed at Boxes situated at the mileage given below, and in the undermentioned Signal Boxes :—

Section—Wye Valley Junction to Tintern.
(One key.) Gang No. 111. 0 miles, 2 chains, to 4 miles 51 chains.

	m.	ch.
Wye Valley Junction Signal Box	0	0
Tidenham Ground Frame	0	70
Box No. 1	1	31
Box No. 2	2	12†
Box No. 3	3	0
Box No. 4	3	65
Tintern Signal Box	4	51

The telephones communicate with the Signalman at Wye Valley Junction and Tintern.

† This box also contains an additional instrument for the blasting key (see instructions on page 76).

Section—Tintern to Monmouth (Troy).
Group A. (One key.) Gang No. 111. 4 miles 51 chains, to 11 miles 46 chains.

Group B. (One key.) Gang No. 71. 11 miles 46 chains, to 13 miles 66 chains.

Group A.

	m.	ch.
Tintern Signal Box	4	51
Box No. 5	5	35
Box No. 6	6	26
Box No. 7	7	11
St. Briavels Ground Frame	8	4
Box No. 8	8	56
Box No. 9	9	35
Box No. 10	10	15
Box No. 11	10	70
Redbrook Ground Frame	11	46

Group B.

	m.	ch.
Redbrook Ground Frame	11	46
Box No. 12	12	32
Box No. 13	13	8
Monmouth (Troy) Signal Box	13	66

The telephones communicate with the Signalman at Monmouth (Troy).

4. Control instruments are provided in the Section between Tintern and Monmouth (Troy).

5. When occupation keys for groups 'A' and 'B' have been withdrawn simultaneously, the Ganger who restores the occupation key first must remain at the box where the occupation key has been replaced, until informed by the Signalman at Monmouth (Troy) that the electric train staff instruments have been tested, and that everything is in order.

6. Before closing the Signal Box each night, the Signalman must place the occupation key in the box provided for the purpose outside his Signal Box, in order that the key for each respective group may be available for the use of the Ganger for the inspection of the line on Sundays—when required, and at any other time when it may be considered necessary, or desirable, to do so. The keys will be placed in the boxes by the Signalman as under :—

Signal Box.	Section for which occupation key must be withdrawn.
Tintern	Tintern and Wye Valley Junction.
Monmouth (Troy)	Monmouth (Troy) to Redbrook portion of Monmouth (Troy) and Tintern Section.

After the last train has cleared the Section, the person in charge at St. Briavels must, in conjunction with the Signalmen at Tintern and Monmouth (Troy) and in accordance with the standard instructions, withdraw each night the occupation key, and place it in the box provided for the purpose, to be available for use by the Ganger the next morning.

7. An Annett's key is attached to the respective occupation keys at Redbrook, St. Briavels, and Tidenham, to enable the Ganger to enter the Sidings with the motor trolleys when required.

When the Ganger requires to use the Siding points at Redbrook, St. Briavels, or Tidenham, he must insert the Annett's key attached to the occupation key, in the Ground Frame. After unlocking the Ground Frame and opening the Siding points, the Annett's key cannot be removed until the points have been placed in the proper position for trains to pass upon the Running line, and securely locked so as to prevent vehicles passing from the Sidings on to the Running line.

Extract from the 1943 Working Appendix.

For Cyril the first 45 minute trip along the Wye Valley Railway had been completed, the time being 7.58 am. He would then take the train back to Chepstow. A second return journey will be followed by a third, at the end of this last trip the train will return to Newport for disposal of the carriages. The steam engine would then depart for Ebbw Junction to be prepared for the following day's work.

Meanwhile the 2.10 pm train service has now left Newport to do a similar pattern of work to Cyril. All will be repeated, hopefully without mishap, but with one slight difference; on the final journey back to the yard to put the engine to bed for the night the driver has to call in at Severn Tunnel Junction. A report on how much water has been pumped that day by Sudbrook pumping station is needed. This is collected and given to the district superintendent's office as a record of the water pumped from the Severn Tunnel. It used to be approximately 24,000,000 gallons each day.

Mike Rees

In 1950 at the age of 15 Mike Rees left school and got a job as a telegraph boy with the GPO based at Lydney Post Office. He was fond of riding his red GPO pushbike but was also keen to learn telephone engineering as a means of progressing his career. Mr Dukes and Mr Pritchard taught him telephone engineering under the supervision of 'Flash Alf', a postal inspector who always wore a black uniform. At the age of 16 Mike had to sit exams to continue in the engineering side of the GPO.

Meanwhile a friend had obtained a job with the railway in the Telegraph Department but unfortunately was rejected a few weeks later because he was colour blind. With the help of his father, who was also a railwayman, Mike was able to get the job vacated by his friend a few days later. Full of enthusiasm Mike embarked on a life which continued a family tradition, his grandfather, his father and now Mike all worked on the railway.

Mike was based at Lydney in the telegraph section under the 'Wizard', Mr Newman, and was responsible for the signals and telegraphs from Lydney to Monmouth, the Wye Valley Railway section. Mike's main task when he first started was to upgrade the whole telegraph line which was operated by batteries, the system utilised overhead poles. The eighty 1.5v cells connected in a series to make 120 volts in all, and had to be tested regularly. They could give a nasty burn if not done properly as these were topped up or replaced. Most of the batteries were stored under Tintern signal box.

It was at Tintern station one day, that Mike, after checking all the old batteries, disposed of a lot of residue in a nearby field, two days later a farmer found six dead sheep on the spot. Mike was questioned and he got a ticking off. Mike also had to inspect the overhead wires along the route, and replace these where necessary. Using leg climbers and belt to climb the poles he checked all the connections and tested the circuits. It was an exacting job but Mike gradually improved the whole of the telegraph side of the line with the result that everything ran much better and the power used by the batteries was considerably less.

Motorised platelayers' trolley approaches Tintern in August 1962. *Arthur Day*

The signalman looks out from Tintern signal box in Great Western days. In the foreground is a rake of loaded permanent way wagons. *BR Western Region*

Mike travelled up and down the line either by the regular train service or by Wickham trolley if the ganger, Tom Murphy, was on duty. Tom had a great turn of speed towards the local pub's opening times.

On one occasion a passneger train was held up at Tintern for quite a while, because the platelayers, having returned to the station at the end of the day's work, had taken home with them the occupation key which had given them control over the section of track ahead. The train had to wait until a man cycled to retrieve the key. At a later date there was an even longer delay. The train was held in Tintern station again, this time it was due to some cattle entering Tidenham tunnel. Hasty arrangements were made for a light engine to come from Chepstow. The locomotive entered the southern portal of the tunnel and slowly drove the cows out.

As a frequent passenger, Mike still remembers travelling through the 1,188 yds-long Tidenham tunnel which sounded completely different from all the other tunnels he ever went in. Because the floor of the tunnel was solid rock, Mike remembers that the train always passed through with a deafening roaring sound. This was heard best of all when journeying in the railcars.

At Tintern signal box Mike recalls Charlie Jones, with his trim beard, operating the signals and tending his flower boxes hanging from the windows. The signals were operated by a McKenzie frame which one could set into three positions according to the weather: hot, mild or cold. Other personnel included Bert Addis who was the lamp man, he always wore an old fashioned yoke to perform his tasks.

Jack Kyte was also a signalman on the line and used to repair people's radios, in between the trains. Then there was Arthur Jarvis who was a signalman at Monmouth. Charlie Fox the station master at St Briavels station was everyone's favourite being the nicest and most helpful person one could ever meet. He loved his job which he did with energetic enthusiasm. According to Mike, if ever there was a true personality on the railway Charlie was the man.

There was also Bernard Vaughan who worked at St Briavels as a porter-signalman. Yet another Vaughan, Bill, was Mike's counterpart on the Ross-on-Wye to Monmouth section. Bill was a very religious man and kept reminding Mike to keep on the straight and narrow. This applied especially around Monmouth station where the railway staff used to pop into the refreshment rooms run by Mrs Wallett. Cider was to be had here and Bill Vaughan used to warn Mike never to go into this establishment as it led to the road of ruin and evil. The refreshment room on Troy station was fairly small only seating about half a dozen people, it was renowned for staying open quite late after the last passenger train had left, just in case anybody had missed their connection or didn't know the timetable.

One of the platelayers from the Tintern to Monmouth section of the track, Fred (Sam) Beech, liked a regular tipple, and in the cider making season used to disappear for an hour or so, visiting various farms beside the railway. He was an expert cider sampler.

At Monmouth (Troy) station, Ernie Watkins was the station master. He had an important job being in charge of a much bigger and busier station, but Mike always remembers him covered with grime carrying a stirrup pump and shouting to him, 'I've just put out a pole fire for you'.

Signalman Charlie Fox with pointsman at Tintern. *Arthur Day*

Mrs Wallett from Wyesham in Monmouth Troy refreshment room in September 1959.

Arthur Day

Charlie Fox in Tintern signal box in 1953.
Mike Rees/Great Western Railway Museum, Coleford

Being a country branch line railway a few extra shillings could be made along the way by those in the know. The most celebrated method of earning extra funds was the bean stick trade. Here the gangers along the track used to tell the engine drivers that they had managed to cut down a few stakes whilst inspecting the permanent way. A bundle of them were awaiting collection along the route. It must have been a strange sight to see a GWR brake van at the end of the train, pass all too often with a load of 8 ft poles sticking up into the air. Other perks included 'dropped' boxes of fish, plus sheep accidentally killed on the railway - all were sold from the goods sheds. Mike Rees is now the curator of the Great Western Railway Museum in Coleford. The exhibits housed here concentrate on the lines in the Forest of Dean and the Wye Valley Railway where Mike worked and had his fondest memories. The museum has been constructed from the derelict remains of the old Coleford goods shed and boasts a wonderful signal box and 7¼ in. gauge miniature railway.

Gilwyn Rich

Gilwyn or George as he was known on the Wye Valley Railway, worked as a signalman at Tintern station, the only crossing place on the line between Chepstow and Monmouth. It was worked by electric train staff in passenger days and wooden train staff after passenger services finished on 5th January, 1959. George had worked on the station before this, booking parcels amongst other vital duties. Many things came and went on the trains. Although there was a well at Tintern station to obtain water, this was only fit to flush the toilets, it was pumped by hand twice daily into a tank close by the lavatories. Because of this, all the drinking water arrived by train from Chepstow and was delivered in milk churns every morning and afternoon. The churns were rolled out of the goods wagon and along the platform into the station.

Other items that needed rolling were barrels of blackberries and plums dispatched when in season to a jam factory. Canoes came and went on a regular basis. They were sent a few days ahead of the groups who later arrived to pick them up. All had to be docketed and accounted for. Later they were sent back again by train, normally to Lechlade where many were hired.

Another major user was Mr Rowe of Catbrook who dispatched his greyhounds to races all round the country from the station. He then collected them on their return. Whoever was on platform duty at the time had the task of walking the dogs up and down and giving them a little water to drink.

When Ted Light the station porter had a break in between trains he would get on his bike and begin delivering various goods in the town. Sausages, salmon and cakes were the usual fare. These were dropped off at local shops, S. Jones (Butcher) who ordered Palethorpe sausages, Thomas, Abbey Stores, Williams & Cotton who sold Lyons cakes and the Abbey Hotel - they liked the salmon which was wrapped in raffia bags for protection.

GWR lorries also brought and took away goods from Tintern station. Ernie Jenkins had a three-wheeler and Roy Stevens drove a lorry which had a hoop and canvas cover. They picked up and delivered meal and cattle cake which

Tintern signal box.

Gilwyn Rich

This view of Tintern station was taken from a train arriving from Chepstow in September 1959.
Arthur Day

Plenty of staff at Tintern but no sign of any passengers. Guard Stanley Foster holds up the train at Tintern, while Charlie Fox is seen with broom in hand. *Arthur Day*

Ex-GWR pannier tank No. 6430 in the down platform at Tintern with a two-coach passenger train bound for Severn Tunnel Junction.   *B.L. Jenkins*

Once again No. 6430 is on duty at Tintern on an up passenger service. The railwayman on the platform has the train staff in his hand. Further along the platform stands a solitary milk churn.
          Provenance Unknown

Loaded stone wagons stand on the line in front of the signal box at Tintern while an ex-GWR pannier tank performs shunting duties on the up platform road.   *Provenance Unknown*

Pannier tank No. 7427 with a Monmouth-bound goods train on 30th October, 1962. By this date the signal arms had been removed from the signal posts.   *D. Fereday Glenn*

A goods train waits to leave Tintern. Charlie Fox is about to hand the driver the train staff in August 1961.
Arthur Day

Pannier tank No. 9619 shunts stone traffic in the sidings at Tintern station in September 1963.
Arthur Day

was stored at the station in an old shed. It had a wire cage inside but it proved unsuccessful against rats. Cattle pens and a hand-operated crane were located nearby. Other items dispatched from Tintern consisted of pit props brought down to Tintern from the Forest of Dean by the Forestry Commission, potatoes were also another crop loaded into the goods wagons.

The largest amount of freight that came into the station was ballast from Tintern Quarry, loaded wagons were brought to Tintern station and dropped off in the sidings. Meanwhile, the engine went on to Monmouth to return later with the goods train. It then coupled up with the ballast wagons once again going south.

A camping coach was positioned at Tintern. It held six or seven people who usually stayed for a week. Staff who were off duty had the responsibility of making sure the coach was kept spick and span. The task of lighting the oil lamps on the station fell to the afternoon signalman, he also topped up the oil and trimmed the wicks. All the signal lamps from Chepstow to Tintern were looked after by Bill Addis the lampman, including a fixed signal at Turrifs, Tintern Quarry. Elsewhere the guard on the last train of the day used to hang an oil lamp on a hook over the station nameboard.

The up-keep of the track was the responsibility of the ganger, Tom Murphy. He and the other PW men George Parfitt, Frank Jones, Alan Brown, Doug Messenger, Walter Hussey and Eric Morgan had two inspection trolleys, one hand-worked, pumping up and down, and one motorised. It is sad to report that Mr Hussey and Mr Williams unfortunately died in the most serious accident on the Wye Valley Railway. The gang was working on Tintern bridge at the time, relaying the track, they were jacking up the rail when, under pressure of the downward thrust, the floor boards of the bridge suddenly gave way. They fell and were drowned by the waters of the River Wye flowing below.

Gilwyn was the last signalman to set the 'road' for the final train on the Wye Valley Railway when he was at Tintern signal box. Trained by other signalmen on the railway, Charlie Price and Charlie Lewis, Gilwyn always made sure all the levers, brasses, windows and floor were polished. The last station master at Tintern was Ernie Watkins, his relief was Mr Davies.

John Wheeler

John started his railway service at the age of 16 in June 1949, as a junior clerk at Chepstow station, a short while after Nationalisation. He worked in the booking office and goods office until aged 23. John then worked as a temporary summer relief station master (class 3) to cover holidays and sickness, almost at once he received a permanent appointment in August 1956 as station master (class 3) at Redbrook, he was also responsible for St Briavels and Tintern. John was re-appointed to a permanent relief post in May 1957 but he continued on occasions to cover the branch until promoted to the divisional office in Bristol in January 1961. Later he moved to the Western Region headquarters Paddington and BRB headquarters at Marylebone, retiring in June 1988.

John recalls that during his time at Chepstow one of the leading porters was named Teddy Edwards who was always relating his experiences of working at Tidenham as a young porter, dealing with wagon loads of hay being sent to the cities to feed horses.

When John arrived at Redbrook, the staff consisted of one porter, Gilbert Short, who lived at Monmouth and cycled down each morning and a lad porter who lived at Redbrook. Gilbert was responsible for the labelling of the wagons of tinplate that were dispatched to Metal Box factories and for shipment to Newport and Cardiff Docks. There was little other goods traffic at Redbrook, and the passengers obtained their tickets from the guards on the trains.

Gilbert did not have 'green fingers' but maintained the station gardens to a very high level winning several 'Best Kept Station' awards. In the beds alongside the platform and on the embankment opposite there was always a profusion of bright flowers, while the signal box was garlanded with highly scented roses.

In the spring/early summer it was usual for the weed-killing train to spray the line and there were anxious moments when it was due, worrying whether they would remember to shut off the sprays through the station as instructed.

The passenger trains were worked by crews from Ebbw Jn, Newport, with about eight men in the link working. The goods trains, two each way to Monmouth, were worked by Severn Tunnel Junction drivers, firemen and guards (the latter acted as shunters at the local sidings). One of the goods guards was Graham Powell.

The staff at St Briavels consisted of two porters who operated the crossing gates, there was little activity there other than pit props being sent by the Forestry Commission to South Wales collieries, sugar beet being sent for processing and the occasional wagon of coal for the local coal merchant. Two churns of milk were sent each day from Whitebrook Halt to the dairy at Chepstow.

Tintern was the busiest of the stations, being the crossing point for all trains on the branch and also the stone traffic from Tintern Quarry was worked into Tintern goods yard before being sent down to Chepstow. There were three staff at Tintern, two signalmen, Charlie Fox who had previously worked at St Briavels, George Rich who lived at Devauden and later worked at Portskewett. The porter, a local Tintern man, was Ted Light. The parcels traffic included packages containing Wye salmon.

The upkeep of the track was the responsibility of a ganger, Tom Murphy, and two or three lengthmen who travelled the line on a small motorised trolley which could be removed from the track at the lineside for trains to go through.

There were only a few minor mishaps during John's time on the branch. Sometimes a wagon would derail in station sidings and occasionally problems occurred with the diesel railcars that were introduced to the passenger service - they were a very popular ride for the passengers and were known as the 'Elver Expresses'. One was No. 13 and the other was No. 4, you would have expected that No. 13 would be the problem one but not so. No. 4 was an old express car that had operated on the Cardiff to Cheltenham service that went through Chepstow about 11.35 am. It was designed as an express unit and had a second engine that only cut-in when a certain speed was reached. With all the branch stops on the Wye Valley Railway, the cut in speed was never achieved, consequently the fly-wheel on the first engine overheated and the diesel often had to be rescued by one of the tank engines working the quarry trains.

The one major mishap was the derailment of the Saturday morning freight train at St Briavels. Because of the siding layout at St Briavels it was normal to shunt the sidings on the return trip from Monmouth - on this particular occasion the train crew were anxious for an early finish and decided that if they cleared the traffic on the trip to Monmouth, they would be able to get back to Wye Valley Junction before the passenger train rather than wait to cross it at Tintern. The problem was that in order to perform the shunt as they wished it was necessary for the engine to run-round its train through the goods siding. There were two levers in the crossing cabin which were operated by a staff given to the crossing keeper by the engine driver. It was necessary for the crossing keeper to take the staff to unlock and operate the points at one end of the siding to let the engine in and then take the staff to unlock and operate another set of points, these also opened the crossing gates to let the engine out. Unfortunately the speeding engine got to the second set of points before the crossing keeper was ready and the engine crashed through the points and the crossing gates. They didn't get an early finish after all!

John's father, Edward John Tamplin Wheeler was station master at Tintern in the early 1930s. Earlier in the 1920s Edward Wheeler lived at Tintern and travelled to Monmouth school, with his brother Ivor and cousin Douglas, by train daily. After leaving school he looked for work and found an appointment at Monmouth Troy booking office. He stayed there until 1923 when he was posted to Abernant and later to Aberfan where he met and married John's mother. In 1929 he was posted to Tintern station as booking clerk under the then station master, Mr Davies.

In the later 1930s and up to 1939, the station master at Tintern was Matthew Muldowney, an unmarried man who did not require the station house. John's family lived in the station house at Tintern until it was required by the next incoming station master, Ernie Watkins, subsequently Mr Watkins was appointed as station master at Redbrook. In 1956 Mr Watkins was promoted to Monmouth and John took over at Redbrook. Up to the time of closure the station master at Chepstow, Mr Goddard, took over responsibility of the Wye Valley line up to Tintern, Mr Watkins the remainder of the railway to Monmouth.

On the lighter side, John had a suspicion that a shotgun was carried on the freight train and that an occasional pheasant was bagged.

One lady, a Mrs Hunt, travelled each week to Newport market with a large basket of garden produce. It was said that she had her late husband's ashes put into an egg-timer 'to get the b. . . . . . to do some work, which he never did when he was alive'.

A regular customer was a Mr Freeman of Brockweir, who used to send exhibits to the Fur & Feather Show on London, regrettably one day one of his prize rabbits was put in the parcels van at Tintern, without it being realised that a greyhound, without a muzzle, was already in transit. The greyhound won! A little poem was sent to Mr Watkins who was at Tintern at the time; the final lines were, 'You really must get out of the habit, of putting the dog too near the rabbit.'

A view looking down onto the Chepstow end of Tintern station. The camping coach can be clearly seen in this 1956 view. *Granville Williams*

During the 1950s, in the months of April and August, special trains used to arrive for the annual races. Some 12,000 birds were released from Monmouth Troy station.

John reckons his Wye Valley Railway posting came about 40 years too soon to take full advantage of the river fishing. His fly rod was always at the ready at Redbrook station, and therefore he was quick to get a good spot on the bank when the fish started rising. The gong on the push-pull train came in very handy when fishermen were walking along the line with their backs to the train.

An extract from the *Monmouthshire Merlin* in 1923 mentions the retirement of Mr H. Davis, the Redbrook station master after 39 years service. To mark the occasion an enjoyable 'social was held at the Redbrook Institute, presentations were made to Mr and Mrs Davis and many speeches were made praising the well-earned respect with which the station master was held by senior staff of the railway'.

Eleanor Fox

In 1937 Eleanor Fox went on holiday with her relations, she writes:

Our GWR camp coach No. 9898 was booked from August 21st-28th, but in essence 'that holiday feeling' got underway the previous week when my mother received a reply to her preliminary letter from the station master of Tintern station. Dated 16th August, 1937 and written in a flowing hand with decided panache, came four pages of GWR memorandum pad containing the following heart warming effusion. My family was taken aback by its enthusiastic jauntiness in what were then very formal days. 'My Dear Mrs Fox' it began chattily, no stilted 'Madam' from *our* station master.

'I am hastening to answer your very interesting letter, just received, and to tell you how awfully happy I shall be in carrying out your wishes expressed within.

By the time your train arrives at our little station, I shall have the coach properly prepared after the departure of the previous tenants, kettle boiling, plenty of fresh (spring) water in readiness, plus an adequate supply of paraffin and methylated spirits.

In addition to the items mentioned in your letter I shall ask the dairyman to leave six or a dozen eggs. I am so hoping you will have suitable weather during your forthcoming visit thus enabling you to explore our beautiful and delightful valley in all its glory.

Finally I mention how particularly pleased my staff and self will be in placing our selves at your service during your stay with us.

I wish you a cosy and comfortable journey when travelling down next Saturday, I feel sure you and your party will especially enjoy the run between Chepstow and Tintern in our streamlined railcar.

Allow me to remain
Yours faithfully
Andrew Muldowney'

I wish I could remember whether we found six or a dozen eggs on our arrival, but Mr Muldowney was as good as his word welcoming us warmly and supplying our all female group with one, not hitherto mentioned, but essential item . . . the *huge* key of the Ladies', 'freedom of the station' indeed.

We settled in happily, there was a twin-bunked bedroom and a four-bunked compartment. I can remember the unexpected height and also the narrowness of the top

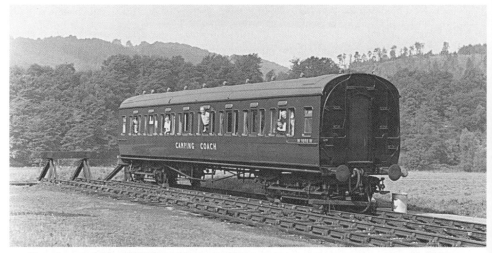

Camping coach No. W9898W at Tintern in 1956. *Granville Williams*

A family group pose outside their camping coach at Tintern in 1956. *Granville Williams*

bunk. I think the mattresses were stuffed with straw, they seemed to me to have a distinct camber.

The windows were the kind lowered by straps and meticulously cleaned every day, they were sparkling. This proved embarrassing on one occasion. We had the habit of merrily emptying the dregs of our cups out of the nearest window. That was until one day 'someone' hurled theirs at a closed window and splattered the assembled company liberally with tea leaves. If only it was left dirty I would have noticed it was shut, was the excuse.

My mother, always one for home laundering, hung her 'smalls' on a string tied between the buffers and found them the next morning full of wood lice. A considerate driver of a steam engine had previously stopped his train short of the station and provided us with an instant supply of boiling water for washing our clothes.

The GWR streamlined railcar, with a cheerful two-note greeting ran up and down the valley three or four times a day and took us north to look around Monmouth and to St Briavels where a pocket-sized castle awaited exploration up a steep hill.

We did a lot of walking during the week, the great loop made by the River Wye at Tintern gave us a long trek to the abbey ruins, these appeared extremely magical on our moonlight strolls. I also recall the evening scenes were lit by hundreds of glow-worms in the hedges.

The train also took us down to Chepstow for the day. I remember resting underneath a very old walnut tree growing on the greensward inside the castle gate. I don't suppose its still there today.

My abiding memory of the holiday though was 'Archibald', a name we gave to a bull amongst a herd of shorthorns grazing in a field behind the signal box. I am sure he was a good tempered beast as he always appeared when we were around, he had an uninterrupted view of the camping coach and could see what was going on all the time in our party of giggling womenfolk. On our last Saturday morning, just before departure 'Archibald' moved up as near as possible to the fence closest to the coach then rolled over and lay down in the grass. With what seemed like pure *joie de vivre*, he kicked his legs up into the air with gay abandon quite unbecoming to his dignity.

I began to wonder if such behaviour in cattle was unusual, however, I prefer to remember this incident as a friendly farewell entirely in keeping with the new found spirit of a lovely week, care of the Wye Valley Railway, and its friendly staff.

Flora Klickmann

Flora Klickmann was possibly the most well known passenger on the Wye Valley Railway during its history, not only was she a famous local author, writing many evocative novels about the era, but she was also the editor of *The Woman's Magazine* and producer of a girls' paper.

In her long list of titles about the Wye Valley she always seemed to find the right words to express our own thoughts and feelings about the natural beauty of the area. Being a literary figure helped of course, but beyond this was inspiration, no doubt this was brought to life by the wonderful views which opened her mind to greater perspectives.

Flora spent half her life in London and the rest of her time in the Wye Valley where she came as often as she could to escape the pressures and noise of the crowded city. A time to think, rest and indulge in different pleasures, such as her little country garden flower patch which meant a lot to her.

Encapsulated below are a few of Flora's dramatic descriptions of the Wye Valley Railway as she once again escaped from London for a short holiday with her companion Virginia, taken from her book *The Flower-Patch among the Hills*.

Station lamp post at Penallt Halt.   *B.M. Handley*

We always consider that emancipation takes place at one exact spot on the Great Western Railway; the only difficulty is that Virginia and I never agree to which is the exact spot.

Virginia insists that the air suddenly changes just beyond Chepstow station, where we change from the London and South Wales main line to the local train that, two or three times a day (Week-days only), runs through our particular valley, like a small boy's toy affair.

This train, which makes up in black smoke for what it lacks of other dignity, steams out of the main line junction with an important snort and rumble; over the bridge it goes, and the stranger would imagine it was well under way. But no; it then comes to a standstill at the point where the main line and the valley line meet, in order that the gentleman who lives - we presume - in the signal box (but who is always standing on the railway line when we see him) may hand to our engine driver a metal staff - some sort of key, they tell me, which is said to unlock the single line railway. I don't pretend to understand the process myself. I only know that our engine driver looks lovingly at it as though it were the apple of his eye (I've craned my head out of the window, that's how I know), and clasps it to his chest, until he gets to the first station on the valley line, where he hands it over to the station master, who, in turn, gives him another one, to which he clings just as pathetically.

In this leisurely way we proceed up the valley.

It wouldn't have any deep significance, but for the fact that Virginia maintains it is the first key that unlocks the imprisoned ego within her, and sets her soul free from the trammels and shackles and cobwebs and chains, hampering, warping, and enmeshing her, that have been riveted by the blighting tendencies of London (and a lot more to the same effect). She says she feels the fetters burst directly that key is handed over, for she knows then that the train is beyond the possibility of making a mistake and getting back on to the London main line again instead of the single pair of valley rails.

Then it is that the air becomes fresher than ever. The primroses that grow all up the rocks, just beyond the signal box, are very much finer than those on the junction side; the Sweet Betsey (alias red valerian) starts to drape the ledges with rosy-crimson as soon as the signalman walks back up the wooden steps to his cabin. And Virginia herself becomes a different being, though opinions are painfully divided as to whether the change is for the better or for the worse.

She says she feels just like the Lord Mayor, or the Speaker in the House of Commons, with a myrmidon going on ahead of her bearing the mace.

We just let her talk on when she gets light-headed like this. After all, this Rod of Office which the engine driver cherishes is what Virginia waits for through four hours of express train - six if you go by a slow one. And the spot where he receives it on the line is where she develops a beatific smile of wondrous amiability.

For me, the chains snap a little further on.

After the driver has received his Key of Office the train meanders peacefully through West Country orchards, placid meadows, and tawny-gold cornfields: past grey-brown haystacks; past little cottages, each with its pig sty and scratting hens, and a clothes line displaying pinafores and sundry other garments only mentioned *sotto voce* in the paper pattern section of ladies' papers. Small, hatless, yellow-haired children, gathering daisies or cowslips in adjoining fields, wave at us as we go by.

Then the engine braces itself for a mighty effort, and gives a business-like shriek on its whistle (this is the great exploit of the whole journey) as it plunges into a very long, dark, clattering tunnel, cut through solid rock. Here we sit in the breathless darkness for several minutes, to emerge finally upon the scenery so unlike that we left behind at the entrance to the tunnel as to suggest that we had entered another country.

Gone are the cornfields, the gentle undulations, gone the farms and cottages, the hayricks and barns. Almost sheer precipices the rocks rise up from the rushing winding river in the valley below, clothed from summit to base with forest trees. The train, now an insignificant atom on the face of nature, puffs vigorously along a ledge cut halfway up the face of these giant hills.

From the windows on one side of the train you look down upon a world of rocks, trees and water, to the horse-shoe bend, where the river turns and twists and doubles back on itself again. Not a house in sight.

The windows on the other side show more grey rocks rising up out of sight, with trees growing where you would scarcely think they could find root-hold, much less food to live and thrive on. And where it is bare stone, and there are no trees, the scarred and jagged surface of the rocks - due to faraway earth-rends and more modern rock slides - is lovingly swathed and festooned with trails of Travellers' Joy and ivy and bryony; while ferns and foxgloves, wild strawberries and Mother of Millions flourish on the narrow ledges, and sprout out from sheltered crannies - such a mist of delicate loveliness veiling all that is grim cold and hard.

Even the wooden posts, from which wire is stretched to fence off the railway company's land from the adjoining woods, are entirely covered with a living mosaic of small-leaved ivy, patterned, with no two scrolls alike, in a way that human hand could never copy.

Below there is always the river, that swirls and rushes noisily at low tides over its weirs. A heron stands motionless on a grey-green moss-covered boulder near a bank. He looks up at the little train; but it is too far away to worry him. He, and a kite circling high overhead, are the only signs of life to be seen as one passes along. Yet the whole earth is teeming with small folk, furred and feathered; the rarest of butterflies are glinting over the rocks; the otter is hiding down in the river pools; and from time to time a salmon leaps into the air, a flash, a streak of silver, and a series of eddying ripples - that is all.

This is the spot where, for me, a new life begins; where unconsciously I draw my breath with a deep intake, and suddenly feel the past slipping from me; the noise the din, the sordidness and care of the city fade into the background and become nothing more substantial than remote nightmare.

Here in this valley of peace and quietness my dreams become realities. And best of all, here God seems to lay His hand on tired heart and tired brain; and I find myself saying. 'This is the rest wherewith ye may cause the weary to rest, and this is refreshing'.

Flora Klickmann died in 1958, aged 91, and is buried at the Moravian church in Brockweir. Maybe one day her books will, once more, be given the credit they deserve.

Eric Broom

Eric Broom came to Severn Tunnel Junction in April 1962 having just gained promotion from engine cleaner at Taunton in Somerset. He was only 16-years-old and had wanted to go to Southall shed in London, but his parents were not too pleased about him living on his own in such a big city at such a tender age. So he arrived at Severn Tunnel Junction with three other young firemen and stayed at the railway hostel close to the station.

His first impression was that the hostel was something of a 'dump' but after closer inspection and the sudden realization of freedom, it didn't seem so bad. There was a snooker room, TV room and a canteen open 24 hours a day. This included a call book where you put your name and time down for a call by the porter, and were sometimes dragged out by the leg in time for work. There was also a sandwich book in which you could order snacks for work.

The bedrooms were tiny with just enough room for a single bed, small dressing table and a built-in wardrobe. There was a communal bathroom but no showers, and a laundry room for washing, drying and ironing clothes. However, the best part was the railway association club next door, where they were quite happy to serve someone of 16 years of age with alcohol!

He immediately found himself on a set of duties or 'turns' which included 'the Chepstow pilot', a freight turn along the Wye valley from Chepstow to Monmouth. The Chepstow pilot would depart from Severn Tunnel Junction at about 6.30 am, shunting would take place at Chepstow preparing the train for Monmouth followed by the mandatory cooked breakfast. Harry (Duckie) Williams was one of the regular guards on this train and Charlie (Hawkeye) Hawker was the resident shunter at Chepstow. The leg pull and banter between these two characters was something to witness and behold. After leaving Wye Valley Junction it was a stiff climb up to Tidenham quarry and then through Tidenham tunnel, downhill to Tintern quarry. The crew would deposit empty ballast wagons at the quarry and take loaded ballast on to Tintern station and would collect them on their return.

It was on this return journey that the most arduous part of the trip could be encountered. With loaded ballast wagons and whatever was brought from Monmouth, a rather heavy train would be assembled at Tintern. Although the pannier tank engine would be running bunker first, if the speed in Tidenham tunnel dropped significantly the crew would be engulfed in the cab by the choking hot sulphuric exhaust of the engine. The very tight clearance in the tunnel both at the chimney and side clearance did not help and passing under the air shaft was welcoming as you knew you had not much further to go before you breathed fresh air again. The footplate crew would lay sand from the engine on the trip to Tintern so they could have sand available on the return journey going up the gradient, however, if the locomotive did break into a slip then it was no fun!

Apart from the tunnel it was always an enjoyable trip up the Wye valley and if a visit from the weedkilling train was long overdue, it was like driving along a country lane with the track invisible below the weeds and vegetation. Sheep or fallen trees were often encountered and flooding was also experienced especially south of Llandogo when winter rains and high tides coincided. On one occasion, after the passing of the train to Monmonth, the permanent way gang railed their Wickham trolley to work on the line, but what they didn't know was that the engine and brake van was to return from Monmouth immediately to collect some more wagons from Chepstow instead of returning later in the day. They met in a head-on collision near St Briavels station, the gang jumped to safety. The trolley was dragged clear and rusted away in the hedge for many years.

Attached to the single line staff was a bunch of keys, some of which were used to unlock the level crossing gates across the A466 road at St Briavels station. Here Eric would open the crossing gates then hang the staff and keys on the crossing post, rejoin the locomotive and then cross the road with the train and stop to enable the guard to close the gates, rejoin the train and give the 'right away' by holding the staff up. One day, on initial approach to the crossing, the driver failed to stop and wrapped both gates around the engine. Luckily, no road users were harmed. On his return to the shed at Severn Tunnel Junction he was asked by the foreman what had happened. He said, 'I had the whip out to that engine but it just wouldn't jump the gates!' What the foreman did not know was that the driver had spent too long in Mrs Wallett's refreshment room in Monmouth Troy station, where strong cider was readily available, and Duckie Williams, the guard, was doing the driving!

The Wye Valley was always beautiful, especially in the autumn with the golden leaves on the trees and the winter time was equally magical. Snow, frost and ice made it a winter wonderland although making railway operations difficult, as in the winter of 1963, after closure to passengers, when the line was blocked by snow and a locomotive fire had to be dropped at Monmouth.

Eric has fond memories of Whitebrook and of Dick and Dulcie Vaughan who lived in the railway house close to Whitebrook Halt. He met them through his wife to be, Jackie Crimp. They acquired the railway house from Dulcie's first railwayman husband, Ted Rosser, who had sadly died. Ted and Dulcie had previously lodged with Jackie's parents, Jack and Nora Crimp, at the Laurels in Rogiet. Eric would line up large lumps of coal on the footplate and throw them off as he went by, then stop on the return journey to pickup eggs or beans. Dick was not too pleased one day when a large lump of coal almost demolished his beans. Before this time Eric's wife, Jackie, has memories of travelling to Whitebrook from Seven Tunnel Junction on the railcars and autotrains. As a young girl she remembers riding on the last train in January 1959.

Beansticks were often cut to order at Redbrook. Eric can remember alighting from the engine near Redbrook and chopping several bundles of beansticks from the woods and dragging them down to the overbridge near 'The Bush' public house. He would always ensure he had half a pint of beer in his glass and sat near the door as when he heard the engine whistle it was a mad scramble up the embankment.

Eric was detailed as fireman on the last scheduled freight train on Saturday 4th January, 1964, Bill Thomas being the driver and Harry (Duckie) Williams was the guard. They departed from Severn Tunnel Junction before dawn, marked by a few fog signal detonators exploding under the wheels of pannier tank No. 7427. Bunting flags were also draped on the engine. After the usual shunt at Chepstow they left for Monmouth with extra brake vans to accommodate passengers, who included several members of the Monmouthshire Railway Society and also Phil Williams (fireman) and Lou Jenkins (guard) who both had fond memories of the Wye Valley line. Charlie Hawker just had to come along. All the way to Monmouth they saw many photographers and some local people to see the last train in spite of it being a bitterly cold day.

On arrival at Monmouth the necessary shunt was performed to prepare for the return journey, followed by the compulsory visit to Mrs Wallett's refreshment room. Eric can remember well the marble top counter and barrels of rough cider. Departure from Monmouth Troy station was witnessed by many people and more detonators as they climbed towards the viaduct and bridge over the River Wye and on towards Chepstow. At Redbrook the train was greeted by yet more detonators and a row of pint glasses of beer from 'The Bush', lined up on the signal box steps. It was at this point in the proceedings, that an off-duty member of the party had had enough to drink and was placed on an upturned bucket in the corner of the cab of No. 7427.

So they steamed on down the valley, through Llandogo, Tintern and on to Chepstow with a rather sad mood descending on everyone with the thought that this really was the end of the Wye Valley line. Although it was not actually the last train to Monmouth, as Eric was fireman the following day of the first train on a Sunday for many years. With a permanent way gang, they recovered some scrap metal and reusable equipment. A further train operated about a week later to return from Monmouth with empty wagons which had been left loaded with coal on 4th January.

It was the condition and cost of maintenance on the river bridges that was the Achilles heel at the time on this line, 5 mph being the speed limit on all of them.

With today's money available through such sources as the National Lottery and much of the trackbed still in existence, who knows what could be achieved. But then it would mean all new bridges over the river and some deviations around some private dwellings built right on the trackbed. Eric's connections with steam has not ended as now he finds himself as a volunteer fireman on the footplate of steam locomotives on the West Somerset Railway between Minehead and Bishops Lydeard and firing No. 6412, the GWR pannier tank used 'top and tail' with No. 6439 on the Stephenson Locomotive Society's railtour of the Wye Valley on 4th January, 1959.

Pannier tank No. 6412 takes water at Chepstow whilst working the SLS railtour of 4th January, 1959. Although the Wye Valley Railway has now gone, happily this locomotive has survived into preservation on the West Somerset Railway.   *Douglas Robinson*

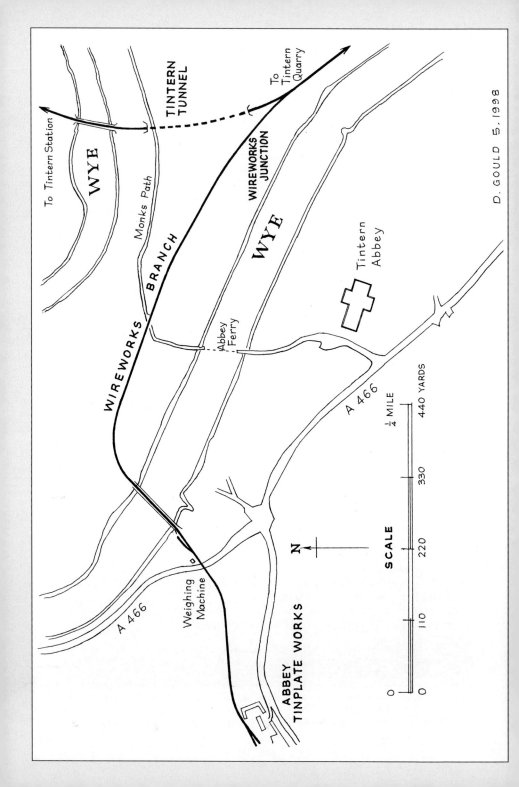

Chapter Nine

The Wireworks Branch
(Tintern Railway)

Tintern and its surrounding area has been connected with metal works from as long ago as 1566 when the wireworks were first founded . Wire and iron work sites were to be found at various locations, from the river bank at Tintern to Pony-y-Saeson, up the Angidy Valley. These various metal works continued for many years, but as iron-making declined a change over to tinplate-making increased and was completed by 1880. Tinplate was to continue to be produced in the Wye Valley for just over 20 years, production ceasing altogether by 1901.

Although metal working had ceased, there was still some industry to be found at Tintern, mainly centred on wood turning, shaping and cutting. The power for the wood works was supplied by the Angidy River, and before the opening of the WVR all goods were carried by boats up and down the river. As already mentioned the Wye Valley Railway was constructed primarily as a north-south link; the alignment of the track was of paramount importance as the fastest route between Wyesham and the Wye Valley Junction was obviously the most direct.

The route finally agreed upon was laid for the greater part on the east bank of the river and effectively by-passed Tintern by going via the second shorter 'tunnel'. The tunnel was cut through a promontory of land that projects westward and is situated across the river from village. The line emerges from the tunnel for 100 yards or so before eventually crossing the river just north of the village, this meant that station was situated some way out of the village much to the dissatisfaction of the locals and Messrs Murrell and Stothart, lessees of the Abbey Wireworks. But nevertheless it was a sound economical move on behalf of the WVR as the site served not only Tintern but Brockweir as well. (Brockweir was to gain its own halt on 23rd September, 1929.)

With the growing concern over the alignment of the railway, representations were eventually made to the Duke of Beaufort, being the owner of the land, by the lessees of the Wireworks and the people of Tintern to lodge their disappointment at being by-passed by the railway. This action culminated in a formal agreement being signed on 22nd November, 1872 between the Wye Valley Railway Company on the one hand and the Duke of Beaufort and his son the Marquess of Worcester on the other, in which the company undertook to build a branch railway across the river to serve the Abbey Wireworks only. The locals still had to use the official station.

The Wye Valley Amendment Act was passed on 14th June, 1875 (WVR Amendment Act. 38 Vict. cap. LL). The Act contained the following provisions:

1. The line was to be reserved for the exclusive use of the landowners and their tenants. It was to be completed by 1st November, 1874 or with the main line if that was completed before.
2. The company was to 'forever maintain the branch and junction in good repair'.
3. No charge was to be made for goods to or from the Wireworks, in respect of the branch, by the company.
4. All vehicles were to be supplied by the company for the transport of goods to and from the Wireworks.

Wye Valley Railway
Tintern Abbey Tramway Bridge over River Wye

Plan No. 3

To Wye Valley Railway

66'0"

Water

Water

66'0"

High

15'0"

66'0"

Ordinary

Low

ELEVATION

Present Surface of Ground

From Tintern Wireworks

To Railway

MARK   OHW

MARK   LW

DESIGN
S.H. Yockney
3, Queen Square,
Westminster

PLAN OF SUPERSTRUCTURE

20 feet

(FROM AGREEMENT OF 1872)

6" Floor Planking

1¼" Tie Rods

MARK   LW

MARK   MHO

CONSTRUCTION
I.S.C.A. Foundry Co.,
Railway Plant Engineers
Newport

From Works

5. The company was to pay the landowners £3,086 for the land and up to £500 for trees etc. disturbed during construction of the branch.
6. The rails were to be not less than 60 lb. per yard. The maximum gradient was to be 1 in 70. The line was to be level over the bridge and beyond. The minimum radius of the curves was to be 300 ft.
7. The bridge was to be constructed according to a drawing appended to the Agreement, capable of bearing a locomotive and three loaded trucks at least and was to have a clear headway of 15 ft between the ordinary high water mark and the crown of the arches.
8. The branch was not to be or become part of the Wye Valley Railway Company undertakings without the written consent of the landowners.

The Wireworks bridge was designed by S.H. Yockney of 3 Queen Square, Westminster, London. The builders were the Isca Foundry Co., railway plant engineers of Newport, Mon., and the contractor was Messrs Reed Bros & Co. of London. Work commenced on the railway on 5th June, 1874 and the Engineers reported in August 1874 that the borings taken from the branch river bridge had revealed a rock bed about six feet below the bed of the river. One year later on 6th August, 1875, it was reported that the Tintern Abbey branch railway was complete and ready for use. A somewhat enthusiastic statement as the main line would not be complete for another 14 months. There were some minor variations in the finished bridge structure to Yockney's original deposited plan. They were as follows:

1. There were ten diagonally braced girder sections shown on the original drawing of the two outer spans, whereas the bridge as built had nine sections in all three spans.
2. The drawing shows the two stone piers as being perpendicular to the base of the bridge. The stone piers as constructed are angled by about 16° towards the west-east line.
3. The bridge is probably a few feet higher than indicated on the deposited plan. The reason for this was that in 1874 the Board of Trade suggested that the structure should be raised by at least two feet. The WVR agreed to raise the bridge platform by 2 ft 6 in. at a cost estimated at £556 15s.

Unfortunately for the WVR by August 1875 Messrs George Murrall and William Stothart of the Abbey Wireworks had ceased trading. So the opening ceremony was a little deflated. The branch lay dormant until the early 1880s when the works were taken over by Josiah Richards, John Rowland Griffiths and David Williams, collectively known as the Abbey Wire and Tinplate Company. This new venture was short-lived and by 1901 trading had ceased altogether. It was also the end of steam traction on the branch as the privately-owned locomotive was sold in February 1902 during the dismantling of the works. However, traffic did not cease on the branch completely as Messrs J. Jones & Son who owned the sawmills and turnery works in Tintern used horse-powered traction to convey goods between their premises and Wireworks Junction. Traffic continued in this fashion until the mid-1930s when the track had deteriorated to such an extent that reconstruction would have been too costly an exercise.

It will be noticed that the WVR was responsible for supplying the rolling stock used on the branch. In reality the rolling stock was supplied by the GWR as the operating company. There is no mention in the Agreement of any locomotive supplied, in fact throughout the branch line's precarious existence a

The bridge which carried the Tintern Railway over the River Wye, seen here in 1978.

B.M. Handley

The weigh house of the Tintern Railway was still *in situ* in 1978, but is now long gone. It had been built in the winter of 1881/1882. The WVR was able to charge a yearly rent of 10s., the only figure it was able to put in the credit column. In the background the Tintern Railway's bridge, now a public footpath, can just be seen, while in the foreground is the A466 road.   *B.M. Handley*

sign appeared near the junction with the main line forbidding GWR locomotives to enter the branch, with the exception of 10 yards or so that led to a gate which closed the branch when not in use. This sign was in fact contradictory to a statement made by S.H. Yockney to the press at the opening ceremony, when he inferred that the Wireworks branch would enable railway access to village and the abbey ruins for the travelling public.

The motive power for the wireworks branch had a varied and colourful history, it ranged from horse-drawn to steam-powered, although not in that order. In the early 1880s a purchase was recorded by Isaac, Watt Boulton of Ashton-under-Lyme, dealers in second-hand locomotives, from George Murrell & Co., Abbey Wireworks, Chepstow, Mon., for a pair of Kitson-built 2-4-0 passenger tender engines with double frames, fitted with 14 in. x 20 in. cylinders, 4 ft 9 in. driving wheels and 3 ft 6 in. leading wheels. These locomotives had been previously owned by the Taff Vale Railway and numbered and named 33 *Ely* and 34 *Rhymney*. Boulton refers to the purchase as one complete locomotive and one part dismantled, being used as a stationary power source. The complete locomotive was re-named *Tintern*.

The later and less conventional form of steam traction owned by the branch and operated by the new lessees, the Griffiths, Richards, Williams Partnership, was known locally as the 'Coffee Pot'. It would seem to have taken the form of an 0-4-0 vertical-boilered locomotive, having a large covered cab and two vertical outside cylinders. It was capable of hauling six loaded wagons at a time. With the absence of a run-round loop at the junction a push-pull method was in use. One story told about the 'Coffee Pot' locomotive involved its driver William 'Bill' Roberts, who was told of the news of the relief of Mafeking (17th May, 1890), at which point he decided to open the whistle full blast and left his footplate there and then, leaving dear old 'Coffee Pot' to blow off its steam, while Bill spent the rest of the day celebrating the good news.

From the opening day the railway or Wireworks branch was to prove a veritable millstone around the WVR company's neck, as no tolls or charges could be made for its use and the operating company, the GWR, refused to take any responsibility for the upkeep and repair. The branch itself was finally made useless by the intense heat of the summer of 1935 which buckled the rails, they were subsequently lifted and sold in 1941. The junction with the main line was the last part to be removed in January 1945.

The maker's plate on the Tintern Railway's bridge over the River Wye.   *B.M. Handley*

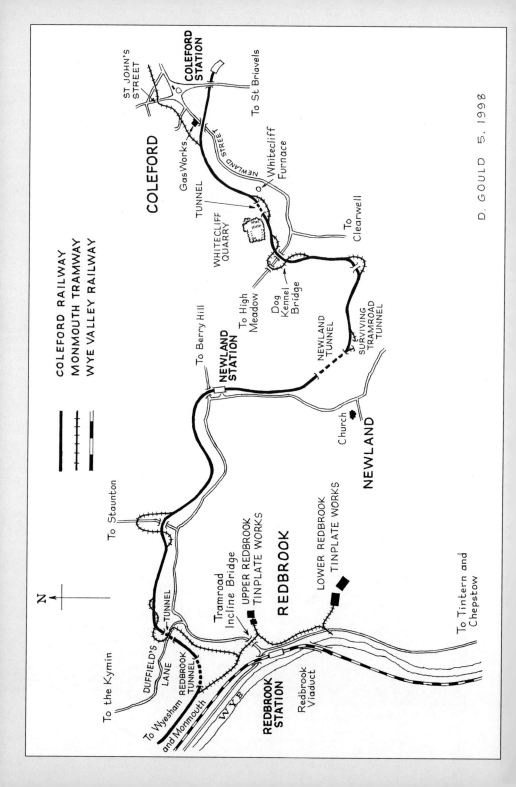

Chapter Ten

The Coleford Branch

The shortest-lived standard gauge railway in the lower regions of the Wye Valley was the GWR branch known as the Coleford Railway. It was opened from Wyesham Junction to Coleford, a distance of 5 miles and 20 chains, on 1st September, 1883 and was owned and built by the Coleford Railway Co. and worked by the GWR from the opening date. The GWR took over the company entirely in 1884 (47 and 48 Vict. cap. 235). Sir Daniel Gooch was appointed Chairman of the new company. The authorized capital was £66,000 in £10 shares. The contractor was Reed Bros & Co. of London, whose Engineer was Arthur Stannard. Lancaster Owen was the Coleford company's Chief Engineer and J.W. Mathews the Resident Engineer.

The Coleford Railway was the fourth branch line to run from Monmouth Troy station and was intended to take advantage of the Forest of Dean's natural resources, i.e., coal, ore and timber, the objective that the Coleford, Monmouth, Usk & Pontypool Railway (CMUPR) had failed to reach (*see Appendix Two*). The line superseded the old Monmouth Tramroad (*see Appendix One*). Stations on the new line were built at Newland, also known as Cherry Orchard, and Coleford.

The first train, consisting of three coaches and a brakevan, left Monmouth Troy station at 8.25 am with Mr Carlisle in control of the locomotive. The engine had been decorated with evergreens and bunting to celebrate the occasion. A few passengers saw the train away in silence. However, along the line 'little groups of rustics' showed their appreciation by lustily cheering and waving hats. The train steamed into Coleford shortly before 9 am, where a large crowd cheered the train as it approached the platform. Seventy passengers, mostly joy-riders, had tickets for the return journey, they were all showered with rice before departure to wish the railway success for the future. Unfortunately this fertility rite proved to be ineffective.

The following description of the Coleford Railway was given by F.W. Arrowsmith at the time of the line's opening:

This railway has been constructed to provide direct connection by rail between Coleford and Monmouth. The length of the line is slightly over five miles, and its course lies through the Whitecliff and Upper Redbrook valleys, and terminates at Wyesham, in the valley of the Wye, where it joins the railway from Chepstow to Monmouth. The line is somewhat interesting from a geological point of view, on account of the number of different strata cut through in its course, consequent on the line being situate, approximately, on the edge of the Dean Forest basin where the coal measures come to the surface and die out. The new station at Coleford is built on the clay which runs under and through the coal seams of the Forest of Dean. This new station forms the terminus of the Coleford Railway, and adjoins the station of the Severn and Wye Railway, but is not at present connected therewith.

Starting from this point the new line immediately passes under a peculiar iron girder bridge, which carries the public road from Coleford to Lydney over it. From this bridge

Contractor Reed Bros & Co. use their locomotive to carry distinguished guests along the Coleford branch on opening day, 1st September, 1883. The train is seen arriving at Newland station.   *Rod Dingwall Collection*

Station master Mr Gosling is seen at Newland station with his family and staff in this 1890 view.
                                                                                                    R.K. Blencowe Collection

the line inclines downwards, and continues to do so more or less sharply throughout its length, reaching at its other end a level of over 450 feet below that of Coleford station. After passing the bridge just referred to the line is laid in a deep cutting, in which the strata next below the coal measures outcrop in singular disorder. The line is then carried across the upper end of the Whitecliff Valley on a high embankment, crossing the Newland Street on a high single-span skew bridge of stone or brick. The Coleford Gas Works adjoins this bank on the right, and a part of the town may also be seen higher up. A rapid curve on the bank then quickly carries the line directly away from the town.

For another quarter of a mile the line is carried along the hillside in a direction parallel to the Redbrook Road, but high above it, affording a more pleasing view of the immediate district than that obtainable from the highway. On the left are here seen some old lime kilns and ironworks, erected in the days before railways had opened out more accessible districts and given them the power of killing the trade at this spot by their competition. The line then curves into a short tunnel, cut through solid mountain limestone, and emerges into a deep cutting partly through limestone and partly through lias clay. An immense quarry lies above this cutting on the right, which has been excavated to supply stone for burning in the numerous lime kilns formerly worked here, many of which are still standing, but now cold and deserted. It is hoped that the construction of the Coleford Railway so close to this excellent limestone quarry will make it possible to put these kilns at work once more.

From the point now reached a fine view is obtained down the valley as far as its bend, and the country is seen to be of increasing beauty as the line approaches Monmouth. Leaving the lime kilns behind, and winding through a short cutting in clay and white limestone, the line comes abruptly upon a high embankment which carries it by a short curve across an arm of the Whitecliff Valley, down which runs the old road from Newland to Coleford. A long massive bridge of stone and brick carries the heavy bank over this road; while on the right a relic of the humble tramway - predecessor of this railway - is seen in the shape of the little bridge which carried its rails across the road at a point higher up the valley. The railway after passing up this embankment - which is about a mile from Coleford station - cuts off a corner of Bircham Wood, and continues its course along the hillside for another half a mile, when, with a sharp turn to the right, it sweeps rapidly round through a deep cutting and under a handsome little stone bridge, and suddenly brings into view the picturesque village of Newland, together with the finest part of the Lower Redbrook Valley. The spire of Clearwell Church and part of the village can here be seen, lying about a mile to the left. Less than half a mile further on the line, after having been carried down the hillside on a long embankment, enters by a sharp curve another deep cutting conducting it into a tunnel 280 yards long, which carries it under the ridge which here separates the Upper Redbrook Valley from the Whitecliff Valley. On leaving this tunnel a glimpse is obtained of Bircham House on the left; and a little further on the famous Newland Oak may be seen, on the same side, about a quarter mile distant.

After a short run through a red loam cutting the line enters the next station - Newland - two and a quarter miles from Coleford. Here the railway widens into a 'double line', to allow up and down trains to pass each other, and two platforms are provided. The booking offices, waiting shed and goods shed are small shapely structures, neatly built in Forest stone. A goods yard, with the necessary sidings, lies on the right of the passenger station. The road from Newland to Redbrook is close to the railway at this point, and below the station is met by two roads from Staunton on the right, which cross the railway by a level crossing opposite the Cherry Orchard Farm.

From the station the line makes a bold curve to the left and enters the Upper Redbrook Valley, the right slope of which it now follows for some distance. Many pleasing views can be had from the numerous bends on the line down this valley. About a quarter of a mile below Cherry Orchard Farm the mountain limestone is again met with, and

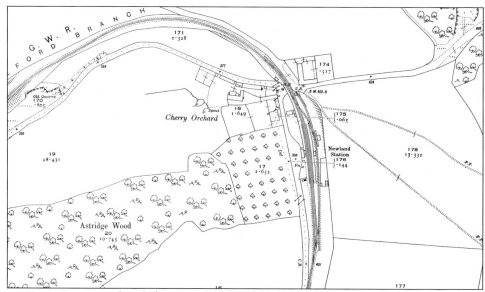

Newland station; although this map is of the 1921 edition rails are still shown as being *in situ*.
Reproduced from the 25', 1921 Ordnance Survey Map

Coleford station (GWR) with Coleford (Severn & Wye) station to the east of it.
Reproduced from the 25', 1921 Ordnance Survey Map

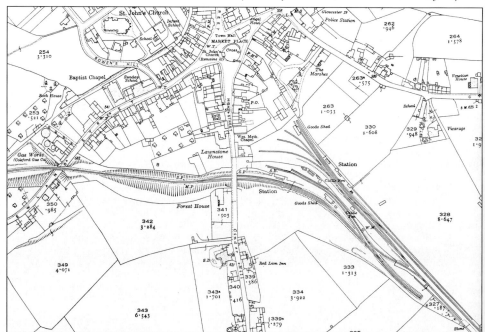

A view of the Coleford Railway looking down the valley from Rocky Lane. A freight train can be seen passing Whitecliff Furnaces.
Pat Bolter

A general view of the railway looking towards Coleford from Whitecliff Furnaces.
Rod Dingwall Collection

Coleford station.   *Paul Smith Collection*

'Buffalo' class 0-6-0ST No. 1640 at Coleford (GWR) station. The train is about to depart with World War I volunteers.   *Paul Smith Collection*

An early 20th century view of Coleford (GWR) looking towards Newland. *Lens of Sutton*

A view of Coleford (GWR) station long after closure to passengers. *Lens of Sutton*

Above: The boarded up signal box at Wyesham Junction in 1922.

H. Rutherford

Left and below: Two views of a derelict Newland station *c*. 1920.

(Both) Rod Dingwall Collection

several old lime kilns are passed on the left, with the well known Swan Pool in the valley below them. After winding through a deep rock cutting the line crosses the Staunton Road Valley - three miles from Coleford - on a high embankment, which is carried over the highway below by a handsome stone bridge of great size and strength. For nearly a mile further the line winds along the hillside, through several cuttings and a short tunnel, till the village of Upper Redbrook comes in sight for a moment, when it quickly bends to the right through a deep cutting in old red sandstone, and enters a curved tunnel about 270 yards long, the other end of which is in the Wye Valley. On leaving the tunnel, the line being at a great height above the river, the beautiful valley of the Wye is seen to great advantage. As the line continues its course toward Monmouth - closely hugging the hillside and gradually falling in level - the railway from Chepstow to Monmouth is seen some 70 or 80 feet below, steadily rising as it approaches the hamlet of Wyesham, where the falling gradient of the Coleford Railway brings that line to the same level as its neighbour. The rails then converge, and the remaining distance to Monmouth - which town is seen in front about a mile distant - is traversed on the rails previously used only by the Wye Valley Railway trains.

From Monmouth to Coleford the line ascended 500 feet over a distance of six miles, on a gradient which varied from 1 in 40 to 1 in 105, the greater portion being between 1 in 40 and 1 in 67. The single line was worked by ordinary staff and ticket and auxiliary block telegraph under standard regulations. The maximum speed permitted over any part of the branch was 20 mph, but a special restriction of 15 mph was imposed over the facing points at Newland, Whitecliff sidings and Coleford; at Wyesham Junction it was further reduced to 5 mph. Here all down goods trains had to stop dead on the loop. The passenger service consisted of two trains each way in the morning, and two in the afternoon Mondays to Fridays, some of these running as mixed trains. The journey took around 20 minutes using four-wheeled carriages.

Throughout its operating life the line never really fulfilled the hopes expected of it and it was closed on New Year's Day, 1917. Some 20 months later most of the track from Wyesham to Whitecliff was lifted and the rails were requisitioned to provide stock for relaying elsewhere. The only exception was just over a mile of track including the passing loops, telegraph poles and signal box at Wyesham, but not the signals. These remained *in situ* for 12 years after the closure and were finally removed in July 1929. The line from Whitecliff Quarry to Coleford was not lifted and continued in use for the transportation of limestone until 1976. Whitecliff Quarry, Coleford, Parkend and the Lydney branch were also closed that same year. Luckily Lydney to Parkend still echoes to the sound of whistles and hissing steam as it is now the location of the Dean Forest Railway.

After the main railway operations had ceased, the tunnel at Newland was taken over for the cultivation of mushrooms. Ammunition was stored here during World War II, and Newland station was requisitioned by the Air Ministry as their local headquarters with the signal box becoming the guardroom. In connection with this military presence the two tunnels at Redbrook were also used as ammunition stores after the ends of both structures had been securely bricked up.

The Coleford branch was the first of Monmouth's standard gauge steam railways to be closed after only 34 years' service.

'16XX' class 0-6-0PT No. 1627 and '57XX' class 0-6-0PT No. 7723 at Whitecliff Quarry, 23rd
August, 1955.   *John Marshall*

Nos. 1627 and 7723 emerge from Whitecliff tunnel *en route* for Coleford on 23rd August, 1955.
                                                                                                                                 John Marshall

Pannier tanks Nos. 1627 and 7723 are seen at Coleford on 23rd August, 1955. Coleford's goods shed can be seen in the background. *John Marshall*

Pannier tank No. 3693 approaches Whitecliff Quarry tunnel on 22nd June, 1964. *F.A. Blencowe*

Whitecliff Quarry as seen from the entrance of the tunnel on 20th August, 1965. Pannier tank
No. 4689 can be seen in the middle distance.   *R.K. Blencowe*

The last steam train working to Whitecliff Quarry leaves Coleford station on 31st December,
1965.   *F.A. Blencowe*

Class '14' No. D9555 about to pass under the Coleford bridge and through the cutting to Whitecliff Quarry on 23rd March, 1967.   *F.A. Blencowe*

Class '14' No. D9555 in Whitecliff Quarry on 23rd March, 1967 with a loaded mineral train.
                        R.K. Blencowe

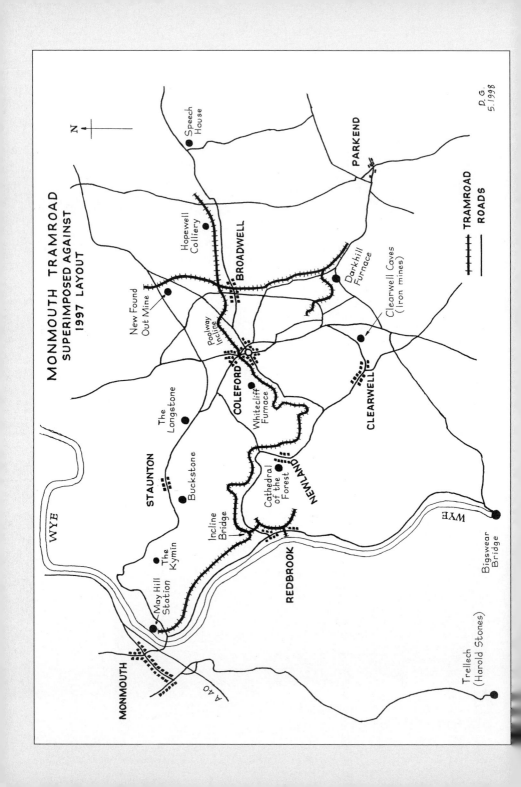

Appendix One

The Monmouth Tramroad

In 1800 the coal in the Forest of Dean going west to Monmouth was being hauled by horses and carts paying tolls at various turnpikes along the roads. To lower transportation costs and speed up supply, a group of interested people gathered in Monmouth in 1808 to remedy the situation. Proposals were put forward which resulted in a Bill being put before Parliament. An Act to build a horse tramroad was granted in 1810. The authorized capital of the company was £22,000 in shares of £50 each with an additional £6,000 if required.

The backers, who included David Mushet, formed the Monmouth Railway Company. In the authorization it was stipulated that the tramroad was to be constructed in three stages. Firstly, rails had to be laid linking the colliers' pits in the Forest of Dean, next came the line from Coleford to Wyesham, and finally the connection to Monmouth at May Hill, in Oliver Parry's yard, by the gasworks, a total length of approximately 8¾ miles.

The Forest sections seemed to have ended at three major locations. One benchmark was Howlers Slade, nearby is Hopewell Colliery which is now owned and run as a Freeminers' Museum by Robin Morgan. Underground trips with cap lamps are very interesting and informative.

Another track went to Darkhill Ironworks. Today stone blocks for securing the 3 ft lengths of 'L'-shaped rail can be found at both locations. The gauge was 3 ft 6 in. At the furnace, David Mushet and his son Robert experimented to discover a method of refining iron ore. These tests led towards the Bessemer process and the modern day steel-making procedures. As such the site is extremely important historically. Nearby Clearwell caves also offer tourists exciting underground trips showing how iron ore was obtained from deep below the earth. To the north the system served New Found Out Colliery and Thatch Mine.

The three tramroads joined together near Broadwell and then continued down towards the Poolway, a rope-worked, self-acting incline, where there was a weighbridge.

In Coleford today 'The Tramroad' north of St John's Street marks the route as it passes through the town's precincts. The permanent way west of Coleford contains many industrial remains which can still be seen today although some have been merged with the later Coleford Railway which tended to follow the same course. The main difference is that the tramroad made bigger loops to avoid building extra embankments, cuttings and tunnels.

At Whitecliff Ironworks, which was worked by David Mushet before his Darkhill projects, the formation passes level with the top of the iron ore and limestone feeding funnel. Beyond the furnace, the Coleford Railway later built a short tunnel to go direct into Whitecliff Quarry, while the tramroad skirted the edge of the hillside.

Further down the valley the tramroad made another deviation, compared with the standard gauge railway, crossing a lane 100 yards away from the Coleford Railway's magnificent stone 'dog kennel' bridge. In comparison, today the abutments of the tramroad's modest bridge are just about standing, its timber spans have long since been taken down.

Further on, hidden in the hillside, under the coffin trail, behind the 'Ostrich' pub at Newland, a village renowned for its 'Cathedral of the Forest' and Freeminers' Brass, is an original tunnel which was used by the old tramroad, this is now partially bricked up to form a doorway at either end. Towards Upper Redbrook the track again diverts from a straight line to run along the contours of a further two valleys, weaving about until it was easier to cross higher up.

Howlers Slade Tramroad with its stone blocks still in place.

Rod Dingwall

On the Mushet Darkhill section looking south, once again stone blocks can be clearly seen.

Rod Dingwall

The Howlers Slade Tramroad passes just a few feet away from Hopewell Quarry which is now a museum dedicated to the Freeminers of the Forest of Dean.   *Rod Dingwall*

The old passageway into Hopewell Colliery. Visitors wearing cap lamps are now taken underground by a new safer entrance. *Rod Dingwall*

Approaching New Found Out Colliery through dense woodland. *Rod Dingwall*

The steep entrance into New Found Out mine. A fan under the chimney helped ventilation by drawing clean air through the underground workings.   *Rod Dingwall*

The remains of Darkhill Furnaces. *Rod Dingwall*

Mushet's Tramroad carried on past Darkhill Furnaces to Easter iron mine, the tramroad nearly reached the old workings at Clearwell. Clearwell 'Caves' have been opened up to visitors and are now a very popular tourist attraction. *Rod Dingwall*

Whitecliff Furnace of 1806. It was here that early experiments into making iron ore more malleable were carried out by David Mushet using charcoal. *Rod Dingwall*

Entrance to the Tram Road, off St John's Street, Coleford. A superb touch by the town planners is the replica tramroad stone blocks. *Rod Dingwall*

The old tramroad bridge on the lane leading to High Meadow. The Coleford Railway's Dog Kennel bridge was later built about 100 yards away down the valley. *Rod Dingwall*

The tower of Newland church, the 'Cathedral of the Forest'. *Rod Dingwall*

The famous Freeminers' brass at Newland church.   *Rod Dingwall*

From the Coleford to Monmouth Tramway a branch led off down the hillside to the Redbrook Tinplate Works. The steep incline crossed the road by a bridge. *Rod Dingwall*

View up the double track incline which fed the Upper Redbrook Tinplate Works. *Rod Dingwall*

A view of Lower Redbrook Tinplate Works in the mid-19th century.   *Rod Dingwall Collection*

The last remaining feature of the illustration above was the old warehouse; since this photograph was taken in 1997 this too has been demolished to make way for a riverside park.   *Rod Dingwall*

Next came another tunnel near Driffield Lane. The lane leads to a lovely country path going up to the Kymin viewing point. Yet again the tramroad and Coleford Railway decided to go their separate ways at this location, the railway building a tunnel a short distance away. The tramroad continued on, until a spur branched away leading to the double-track Redbrook incline in the valley bottom. At its foot is an angled bridge, which is still standing today. This bridge once took coal wagons in to the Upper Redbrook Tinplate Works. Beyond, the tramroad ventured to a wharf, owned by the Monmouthshire Railway Co., on the River Wye. A trailing connection opposite fed the Lower Redbrook Tinplate Works.

Back up at the top of the incline a weighhouse was constructed so that every wagon which passed could be properly weighed and exact records kept of tonnages carried. It was from these records that charges would be calculated, coal, lime, stone, clay (for brickmaking) and iron ore being the main items transported. The Monmouth Railway Act of 1810 is the very first to make specific mention of railway passengers and fares. It stated that 'For every carriage conveying passengers charges are not to exceed 6*d*. per mile'. Rates for agricultural lime and manure was 8*d*.

After the transactions had been completed the tramroad swept around the hillside, to face in a northerly direction amongst trees, before descending to Wyesham and on to its terminus at Monmouth, May Hill.

The tram wagons on the Monmouth Tramroad were of four wheels, not less than 20 in. in diameter. It is recorded that the wagons ran down hills by gravity for most of the journey, horses riding in dandy trucks while descending. Two men controlled the sprag braking system. For ascent six horses were used to pull six wagons. A further two men held the horses' reins.

In forthcoming years the Monmouth Railway changed hands. Firstly it was owned by the Coleford, Monmouth, Usk and Pontypool Railway (1853) (*see Appendix Two*) which wanted to convert it to standard gauge in order to transport iron ore to South Wales, this was to keep the blast furnaces there running. Stocks of iron ore in South Wales were declining fast, and new reserves were needed, while in the Forest of Dean all the minerals required could be found. It was just a question of moving them efficiently. The Monmouth Railway's tramroad was lifted and changed to standard gauge in 1883 by the GWR, becoming the Coleford Railway with a terminus at Monmouth Troy station.

Newland tramroad tunnel measures 8 ft wide by 7 ft high. Today it is a nice warm place for sheep to shelter! *Rod Dingwall*

Appendix Two

The Coleford, Monmouth, Usk & Pontypool Railway

As with most other parts of the country during this period of railway expansion, many fanciful schemes were proposed to run to or through the historic town of Monmouth, none of which materialised until early in October 1857 the Coleford, Monmouth, Usk and Pontypool Railway became the first to reach the then county town. When that title went to Newport in 1974, old Monmouthshire and Newport borough were united to form Gwent. Twenty-two years later Gwent was abolished. Newport became a unitary authority in its own right as did Monmouth borough.

The railway was intended to eventually link up with a tramroad known as the 'Monmouth Railway' (*Appendix One*) at Wyesham on the east bank of the river just opposite the town of Monmouth, consequently allowing the CMUPR access to the rich timber and coal assets of the Forest of Dean.

The CMUPR was authorized by an Act of Parliament on 20th August, 1853, allowing the company to construct a railway from Little Mill Junction on the then Newport, Abergavenny & Hereford Railway (NA&HR), about two miles north of Pontypool Road station, to Coleford with a branch at Dixton giving access to Monmouth gasworks. The section from Little Mill to Usk was the first to be opened on 2nd June, 1856 and was worked by the NA&HR until 12th October, 1857, this being the date of the completion of the line into Monmouth and the opening of Troy station.

When the CMUPR commenced service, passenger and freight trains were operated between Little Mill Junction and Monmouth Troy with the intermediate stations situated at Usk, Llandenny, Raglan Road and Dingestow. But like many country branches, stops were also made where necessary and this became a regular practice at a place known as Raglan Footpath. The reason for this was that the official station was situated some way out of Raglan but as the name 'Footpath' suggests, there was no road connection.

Monmouth Troy on 12th October, 1957. The last train from Pontypool Road, a Stephenson Locomotive Society special is seen on the left, while on the right pannier tank No. 7781 has just arrived from Chepstow. The special train ran on the day of the Usk-Monmouth line's centenary. *Arthur Day*

On the 1st July, 1861 the CMUPR was leased to a concern known as the West Midland Railway (WMR) which had been formed by an Act of Parliament on 14th June, 1860. This company under the Chairmanship of William Fenton involved the amalgamation of the N&AHR, the Worcester and Hereford Railway and the Oxford, Worcester & Wolverhampton Railway.

The time of leasing was significant as it was the date of the first closure on the line at Little Mill Junction station, after which services had run to and from Pontypool Road. However, in 1863 the station was re-opened.

The halts and stations along the old CMUPR route remained the same until 1876 when under the GWR control Raglan station was officially transferred to the one time unofficial stopping place known as Raglan Footpath. The original Raglan station was closed to be later re-opened as a halt on 24th July, 1931. Three more halts were subsequently added, the first in 1927 at Glascoed between Little Mill and Usk, Elms Bridge Halt was next situated between Raglan and Dingestow and opened on 27th November, 1933, and the final halt was Cefntilla opened on 14th June, 1954 between Llandenny and Usk.

During 1861 while under WMR control a short stretch of line was opened across the Wye at Wyesham via a magnificent stone viaduct and iron bridge, thus enabling the CMUPR to fulfil its original plan of reaching the Forest of Dean and taking advantage of its natural resources. The 1853 Act had empowered the CMUPR to purchase the Monmouth Railway's undertakings. Unfortunately due to its leasing to the WMR and eventual amalgamation with the GWR on 1st July, 1863, these options were never taken up, in fact construction of the Pontypool to Coleford Railway stopped short at Monmouth Troy station for passenger traffic and at Wyesham for goods.

The CMUPR closed exactly 100 years after it opened, 12th October, 1957. A centenary train organized by the Stephenson Locomotive Society marked this sad anniversary.

Appendix Three

The Ross and Monmouth Railway

Eight years after the arrival of the CMUPR a second railway company was to drive its metals towards Monmouth, this being the Ross and Monmouth Railway authorized by an Act of Parliament on 5th July, 1865. It took eight years to build and was worked from its inception by the GWR; the contractor was Joseph Firbank, and the line was first opened to passenger traffic on 4th August, 1873.

The station at Monmouth was situated at Mayhill on the east bank of the Wye and was initially a terminal station, as the bridge over the river (which still survives) was not completed for several months after the opening ceremony. On completion of the bridge the line was extended over the river to Monmouth Troy station and was opened to traffic on 1st May, 1874.

There were five stopping places erected along the 12½ mile route, these included three stations which were built during the initial construction of the line situated at Kerne Bridge, Lydbrook Junction and Symonds Yat, and two halts which were added later, the first at Walford which was opened in April 1931 and a second at Hadnock opened as late as June 1951. The Ross and Monmouth was the only one of Monmouth's Railways to remain independent until the 1921 Railways Act forced its amalgamation with the GWR in 1922.

In January 1959 the Ross and Monmouth Railway was served with a closure notice, consequently its passenger service was withdrawn, although goods and freight trains continued for a further five years. The inevitable final closure of the line came in January 1964.

Chronology

1865	First plans of proposed railway drawn up.
13th July, 1866	Reading of Parliamentary Bill (amended plan).
10th August, 1866	Parliament sanctions line.
22nd November, 1872	Formal agreement signed for the building of Wireworks branch.
25th March, 1874	Publication of Prospectus.
May 1874	Construction work commences on Wye Valley line.
June 1874	Construction work commences on Wireworks branch.
August 1874	Wireworks branch completed.
14th June, 1875	Wye Valley Railway Amendment Act passed.
19th October, 1876	Special train carrying officials makes journey along branch.
1st November, 1876	Railway officially opened to the public.
1st September, 1883	Wyesham Junction to Coleford branch opened.
December 1904	Circular from Chairman to shareholders informing them of take-over.
1st July, 1905	Wye Valley Railway amalgamated with the GWR.
1st May, 1909	Bigsweir station renamed St Briavels and Llandogo.
1912	Tintern station renamed 'for Brockweir'.
1st January, 1917	Coleford branch closed from Wyesham Jn to Whitecliff Quarry.
1st January, 1917	Tidenham station closed.
1st February, 1918	Tidenham station re-opened.
11th January, 1927	Redbrook signal box closed.
1st February, 1927	The appendage 'Llandogo' dropped from St Briavels station.
1st February, 1927	Whitebrook Halt opened.
7th March, 1927	Llandogo Halt opened.
30th October, 1928	Tidenham signal box closed.
21st November, 1928	St Briavels signal box closed.
July 1929	Remaining section of Coleford branch at Wyesham removed.
23rd September, 1929	Brockweir Halt opened.
12th January, 1931	Wyesham Halt opened.
1st August, 1931	Penallt Halt opened.
18th July, 1932	Netherhope Halt opened.
1935	Redbrook station renamed Redbrook-on-Wye.
February 1941	Rails lifted on Wireworks branch.
4th January, 1959	Last passenger train to use the Wye Valley line.
5th January, 1959	Line officially closed to passenger traffic.
6th January, 1964	Line closed completely from Monmouth Troy station to Tintern Quarry.
24th August, 1964	Branch worked as a private siding from Wye Valley Junction as far as Tintern Quarry.
1976	Whitecliff Quarry to Coleford closed.
December 1981	Last train through Tidenham tunnel to Tintern Quarry.
September 1992	Last train to Dayhouse Quarry, Tidenham.

Acknowledgements and Bibliography

Thanks are due to John Morris for his valuable contribution with regard to signalling on the Wye Valley Railway. Thanks also to Chris Turner for help with the Third Edition.

First Whistles in the Wye Valley, H.W. Parr
Deposited plans of the Wye Valley Railway, National Archives, Kew
GWR Engines, published by David & Charles
British Rail Motive Power, published by Ian Allan
A Trip by Wye Valley Train, T.B. Peacock (the author, 1948)
Railways to Tintern and Coleford, T.B. Peacock (Locomotive Publishing Co., 1952)
Monmouth to Coleford by Rail, T.B. Peacock (the author, 1947)
The Great Western Railway in Dean, H.W. Parr (David & Charles)
An Historical Survey of the Forest of Dean Railways, Layouts and Illustrations, Peter Smith (OPC)
The Forest of Dean, Arthur O. Cooke
Monmouth and the River Wye in Old Photographs, Monmouth Museum
Chepstow and the River Wye in Old Photographs, Chepstow Museum
The Water Powered Industries of the Lower Wye Valley, S.D. Coates
The Ross and Monmouth Railway, Mark and Celia Glover (Brewin Books)
Secret Forest, Ray Wright
The Wye Valley, Keith Kissack
Tintern's Story, Judith Russell
The Flower Patch Among the Hills, Flora Klickmann
Lower Wye Valley, Visitors' Handbook, Bradley Hill Workshop
The Wye, Black's Guide Books
Like a Tree Planted, The Story of Brockweir Moravian Church, J.D. Monger
Tintern Abbey, CADW
The Old Station, Tintern, Monmouth County Council
Monmouth's Railways, A Historical Survey, W.J.P. Shirehampton
The Buccaneers of America, Alexander O. Exquemelin (Dover Publications, New York, 2000)
www.cavazzi.com/morgan Franco's Cybertemple, the Life and Times of Sir Henry Morgan
www.data-wales.co.uk/morgan.htm Data Wales: Henry Morgan, 1635-1688. A Welsh buccaneer and son of Monmouthshire

The end of the Wye Valley Railway near Tintern Quarry in 1979.   *B.M. Handley*

Index